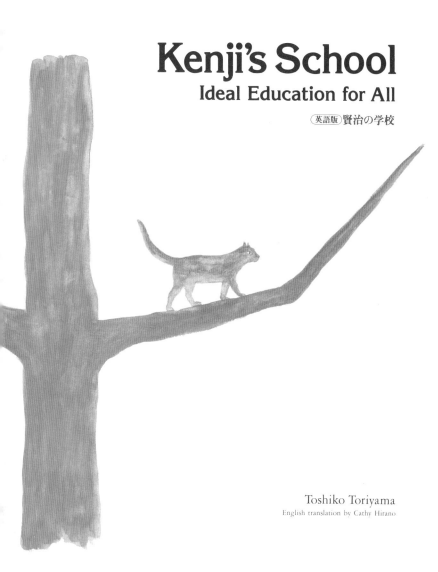

Kenji's School
Ideal Education for All

英語版 賢治の学校

Toshiko Toriyama

English translation by Cathy Hirano

International Foundation for
the Promotion of Languages and Culture (IFLC)

Kenji's School

—Ideal Education for All

by

Toshiko Toriyama

English translation by Cathy Hirano

Kenji's School
— Ideal Education for All

Published by International Foundation for the Promotion of Languages and Culture (IFLC),
Sunmark Building, 1-32-13, Takadanobaba,
Shinjuku-ku, Tokyo, Japan 〒169

Distributed by Sunmark Inc., 1-32-13, Takadanobaba, Shinjuku-ku, Tokyo, Japan 〒169

Printed in Japan
ISBN4-7631-9187-X C0030
First edition, 1997
Book design by Shigeo Kawakami

Introduction

Foreword

Kenji Miyazawa is the best-selling author in Japan today, despite the fact that his literary works were virtually unknown to the Japanese public when he died in 1933. Born in 1896 in Iwate Prefecture, one of the remotest and harshest districts in northern Japan, he was an avid scholar, fascinated by the new ideas, science, and technology that were beginning to filter into the countryside just thirty years after the opening of Japan to the modern world. At the same time, he was profoundly affected by Buddhist scripture, particularly the Lotus Sutra, which he studied and strove to apply in his own life.

The eldest son of a prosperous pawnshop owner, he found it impossible to reconcile his affluent lifestyle with the stark poverty of rural Japan. The lives of the peasant farmers were bleak. A poor harvest, of which there were many, meant famine, and starvation forced many families to sell their children. Kenji's compassion for these people caused him to devote his energy and talents to improving their lot. He studied agronomy and taught at the local agricultural school, only resigning in order to farm and to provide instruction to the local farmers. Until his untimely death at the age of thirty-seven, he continued to express his moral vision, his love of nature, and his compassion for all created things in poetry and stories, many of which he wrote specifically for his students to read aloud or enact.

Although his works were ignored during his lifetime, they subsequently gained great popularity and are included in Japanese public school textbooks. Now, more than sixty years after his death, they have inspired Toshiko Toriyama and other like-minded people to pursue new pathways in education that address the social and moral problems facing Japanese society today.

Toriyama, a schoolteacher for three decades, is known in Japan for her innovative approaches to education both in and out of the classroom. Having experienced firsthand the turmoil of Japanese children trapped within a restrictive and competitive education system, she began a series of workshops to help adults and particularly parents gain a greater awareness of their true selves. This evolved into the concept of "Kenji's school." The name refers not to an actual institution or facility, although one such school now exists, but rather to an educational approach that seeks to transform both the individual and society by reviving the spiritual awareness of our oneness with creation. The study and dramatization of Kenji's writings form a focal part of their activities.

It is important to keep this in mind when reading Toriyama's book because, despite the title, the first two-thirds is devoted to Kenji's life and writings, while the problems in Japanese society and the present education system, and the concept of "Kenji's school" itself, are only taken up toward the end. To a Westerner, this style of organization may seem extremely foreign and even illogical. The book represents, however, an impassioned plea for a change of focus in education and a greater personal awareness that is equally applicable in our own society, and the insights gleaned from Kenji's life and works are offered as an essential part of the solution.

A key term in Toriyama's work is the Japanese word *karada*. Literally translated, this means "body" but I have not used this translation except where it is obvious that the text refers to the physical frame alone. Western speakers of English tend unconsciously to perceive human beings as comprising two separate elements, the physical or body and the non-physical, be it mind, soul, or spirit. In Japanese language or culture, and especially in Toriyama's work, human beings are regarded from a much more holistic perspective. When Toriyama uses the expression "to learn with your body," she refers not only to experiential, hands-on, material education, but to using our intuitive powers and feelings as well.

Accordingly, the translation of this term was a delicate and sensitive task. Depending on the case in which it is used, it would be more natural in English to translate it with words such as "soul," "essence," "heart," "spirit," "inner voice" and "the self." None of these, however, includes the physical aspect nor could they be applied universally throughout the text. I have therefore chosen the word "being" to express this concept. Although it may sound stilted or unnatural in some places, to change it to a more natural-sounding English expression would of necessity imply that the concept of dualism exists in the Japanese text when it most emphatically does not.

Cathy Hirano

Preface

Kenji's school began in the early summer of 1994 as a call to those who want to create a society in which children can aspire to fulfill their potential. It was brought into being by adults who accept that children's suffering, expressed as an appeal through bullying, refusal to go to school, violence, overeating, anorexia, and seclusion, is caused by adults.

Children are gasping for breath. Censured by the common sense dictated by our society, they are compared, crushed, and wounded. Some are so consumed with self-hatred that they turn on their own selves, judging their life to be of no value. The majority of children in Japan today have concluded that people will never be able to live together with trust, respect, or appreciation for one another. They do not believe that we can create a society that will purify the air, water, and soil, and coexist in harmony with nature. They have been divided from their peers in a society that places priority on money, status, honor, and academic achievement, exhausted from phony relationships, and overwhelmed by their own impotence.

Children do not believe that they carry within themselves talents entrusted to them from heaven. I want to create a society in which children will have hope. This is, I believe, our responsibility as adults.

Let us, with all our strength, reach out to these children who have been thrust down and defeated. Let us support them in recovering their true selves, in manifesting their God-given talents, and in becoming people who will do the work of heaven. To this end, let us reeducate ourselves, heal the wounds inflicted on us by society, and be transformed into beings capable of manifesting our innate capacities.

It is not only children who are suffering. Children are merely expressing their parents' pain. It is essential that we fix our gaze on our own selves, deceived by the grind of daily life or labor, and to transform ourselves, inclining our ears to the true voice of our being, hearing within the voice of the galaxy, and living our life in accordance with the will of the cosmos.

This is Kenji's call to us in *An Introduction to Peasant Art* which he wrote in 1926.

The happiness of the individual cannot be attained without first realizing the happiness of the whole world.

To live strongly and truly is to live in awareness of the galaxy within you and to respond to it.

Let us seek true happiness for the whole world; the search itself is the path.

It was people who responded to this exhortation and yearned to put it into practice that brought Kenji's school into being. This school is a place where all individuals can manifest their innate talents, become conscious of their transformation, and aim toward doing "the shining work of heaven."

Although it is possible to talk about Kenji, it is extremely difficult to translate his admonitions into action for this naturally entails the pain of personal transformation and a revolution in consciousness. If we do not prepare ourselves and choose the "stony path," we will never be able to do what Kenji taught. It may not be possible for most people to immediately accept a school suitable to bear the name "Kenji." However, surely this concept which applies the exhortation in *An Introduction to Peasant Art* will spread. The times are rolling inexorably from the mere discussion of Kenji to an age of putting his words into practice.

It is exceedingly difficult to capture on paper this constantly evolving movement, Kenji's school, and I have had to rewrite this manuscript repeatedly. What I described yesterday has already changed by today.

Moreover, having spent the last two years traveling throughout Japan, almost never at home, it has been extremely difficult for me to complete the book, particularly as two-thirds of this time was spent giving workshops in various parts of the country.

Accompanying participants on their journey of suffering, I found it impossible to switch my being into a state conducive to writing. On top of this, manuscripts for the magazine *Kenji's School*, which I edit with Takashi Tsumura, have followed me continuously.

As a result the six or seven book projects that I have taken on remain virtually untouched. That this book was born in the midst of such a situation is due to the strong encouragement of Susumu Takaseki of the Editorial Department at Sunmark Publishing Inc., and editorial staff member Yachio Tanaka and to the support of its president, Keichi Kajikawa. I can never sufficiently express my appreciation.

My ardent prayer is that this poorly rendered text will somehow reach even one of the many who already are, or who are thinking of, putting Kenji's words into action, and that we can work together to create a new age never yet experienced by humankind.

Toshiko Toriyama
February 1996, Kenji's School, Miasa-mura, Nagano
The last day of the first semester

Contents

Chapter 1

SOARING IN SPACE

Happenings

Kenji Miyazawa's written works and his way of life shed light on the direction we must take in order to build a new age. They make us aware of the objectives, the way of life to which our beings aspire.

The first things that surprised me about Kenji were his complete oneness with nature and the incredible sensitivity that welled unconsciously within him. How did he come to be this way? The recollections of his students are invaluable in learning about what kind of being he was and the type of sensitivity he had.

On December 3, 1921, Kenji Miyazawa became a teacher at the district Hienuki Agricultural School (subsequently the prefectural Hanamaki Agricultural School). For four years and four months he instructed his students in such subjects as fertilizer, soil, weather, mathematics, chemistry, and English, in addition to providing practical training in rice cultivation.

What kind of teacher was Kenji to his students? And in what form do their memories of him remain etched in their hearts and beings today?

The vast majority of scenes evoked by his students' recollections portray him consumed by innocent joy, spellbound at the sight of snow, a mountain, or a forest. Yasushi Terui, for example, related to me the following story.

It was a clear day in October. The teacher said to me, "Let's go to the river." So I took him to a place where it

branches off slightly from Kitagami River. The teacher asked me, "Can you handle a boat?" I said, "Sure, if it's just around here," and he said, "Then let's go in that boat."

They did not know whose it was, and Terui, feeling a pang of conscience at borrowing someone else's property without asking, announced, "We're borrowing your boat," before he cast off and began poling.

Well, the water's surface happened to be very still and the sun was shining. And the teacher must have been feeling very good. When we got to the middle of the river, he took out an apple, I don't know where he pulled it out from, and he put it in the water. The sun was shining, you know. And the apple shimmering in the water, well, it was like you see in a prism, the light refracting off it. The teacher did this over and over, pulling the apple up and down. He'd raise it, and say, "Ahhh, that's beautiful!" but each time his voice was different, his way of enjoying it, you know.

Listening to him reminisce, I recalled Kenji's work "*Yama nashi*" (The Wild Pear). A wild pear falls into a river and sinks gently, then bobs back to the surface, the golden dapples on it glittering in the light of the moon. This scene merged with Terui's story in my mind.

Kenji's joy obviously made a deep impression on his student. Terui describes it in this way.

I just can't express in words his unabashed joy. Perhaps you could call it a childlike naiveté, a spontaneous innocence. He was so absorbed in that world, it made no difference if I was there holding the pole and watching him, if anyone was there at all. He and nature were in perfect union.

Listening to Terui talk, I realized how profoundly his teacher's behavior had struck him. Here was an adult unlike any he had encountered before.

In those days, common sense dictated that adults should work the fields where they struggled to eke out a meager living. Yet here was not only an adult, but a teacher no less, who seemed completely oblivious to the rules of his society, bobbing an apple up and down in the water, completely lost and delighting in nature.

The sight of Kenji's joy was a major happening in the life of the youth, Terui. I use the word "happening" because I was strongly impressed by the words of Professor Takeji Hayashi, formerly a teacher at Miyagi University of Education, who insisted that "Any lesson that does not result in a major happening within the student is not a lesson."

Such a happening will never occur if a child is bombarded with information non-essential to his being. Sealed within each individual is the knowledge of what he truly needs, of what his heart, his whole being seeks, that which transcends his worldly desires and machinations. When a teacher's actions or words resonate within a student's being, a happening occurs and the student is filled with wonder.

This is what occurred within the young Terui when he saw his teacher spellbound by nature, overcome with joy.

The common sense that Terui had acquired through daily social relationships probably reflected such ideas as adults must work, rear children, and be regularly employed, but human beings have always been more than this; they have always instinctively sought something else. As "fragments of the stars," we humans contain within us something unfathomable, and I feel that for Terui, Kenji's behavior sparked something within this immeasurable part of his own being.

Kenji's joy as he played on the river was a happening in itself, but that was not the only thing that astonished Terui. Kenji turned to him and asked, "Would you like to go swimming?" October in Iwate Prefecture is cold. Nobody swims in that season. Terui declined the invitation, exclaiming, "Who, me, sir? No, I can't," so Kenji went swimming alone.

> I nosed the prow against the shore. The teacher had stripped off his clothes almost before he got out of the boat and walked into the river. He swam out into deeper water and then came out quickly, blowing hard and announcing happily that it felt great. That was the kind of crazy thing our teacher did.

Confronted with such unexpected behavior, Terui is so flustered, he tells a fib, claiming that he cannot swim. At the same time, some part of Kenji's essence seems to have made a powerful impact upon him.

After graduating from Hanamaki Agricultural School, he went on to the Iwate Prefectural Normal School and became an elementary school teacher. He was forced to retire in 1945 due to tuberculosis, but surely with deep regret because he earnestly wished to impart to children what he had received from Kenji. In 1946, he gathered children from the neighborhood and together with his wife, also a retired teacher, started a drama group called The Kenji Children's Association, which performed Kenji's stories.

The group received its name from a poet, Kotaro Takamura, who had secluded himself on a mountain near Hanamaki hot spring in remorse for his part in World War II. The original purpose of performing Kenji's works was to console Takamura. The latter was thrilled, and, calling the group The Kenji Children's Association, he urged them to continue.

Among many activities, including the establishment of a kindergarten in 1964, Mr. Terui has continued these children's plays for the last fifty years. The group only performs Kenji's stories. I asked Mr. Terui why. "Well, it's partly because I was his student," he replied, "but more than anything because his works are truly beautiful."

Mr. Terui's use of the word "beautiful" summoned up the image of Kenji spellbound by the beauty of the light refracting off the water and the wet apple, as he repeated the word "beautiful," each time with a different intonation.

Since that incident, Mr. Terui has doubtlessly been profoundly conscious of the importance of interacting with his students in the same way, recalling Kenji's figure rapt in contemplation and merging this image with the beauty of his literary works.

One day when Terui was walking with Kenji along a road, Kenji suddenly bounded off into the grass, scrambling through the undergrowth on all fours just as if he were a dog, and howling "ho, ho!" in a strange voice. Then he leapt up and began to dance. Returning to Terui's side, he remarked, "So, what do you think of that? It's fun to walk with me, isn't it?"

Terui's father was also a teacher and he had in fact taught Kenji in the fifth and sixth grades. Terui must have inherited some of his ability from his parent, but he gained something entirely different again through watching Kenji. For Terui, witnessing Kenji's extraordinary behavior was certainly a major happening.

A Heart that Communed with Nature

The memories of Yoshimori Neko, who passed away in August 1995, similarly leave a vivid impression. He relates how he and Kenji lay upon a bed of white clover blossoms in the yard of the newly built school, gazing up at the sky.

The teacher rejoiced from the depths of his soul just watching the white clouds floating across the clear blue sky. He talked to them, calling out "Oi!" "Isn't this great, Neko?" he said to me. He gave no thought to material gain or loss. White clouds drifting . . . there was nothing more than this. This was sufficient.

Lying flat on his back with his teacher, gazing up at the

drifting clouds, Kenji remarking, "Isn't this great?" That was all, but it was seared forever in Neko's heart. The beauty of nature itself and Kenji's naiveté, so far removed from society's calculations of profit and loss, left a profound impression upon him.

Kenji fused with nature, responding spontaneously to its beauty, and he transmitted that pure feeling directly to his students. For example, he often took them hiking up Iwate Mountain to admire its majestic beauty. His enthusiasm was infectious.

When I was making the movie "*Kenji no gakko— Taneyama gahara*" (Kenji's School—Taneyama gahara), which was completed in August 1995, I was privileged to hear the memories of many students. Of these, Neko spoke about what he felt when they went to Taneyama gahara.

Black clouds moved in and thunder rolled. Below us a herd of 800 horses stampeded down the hill, their hooves drumming. That was Taneyama gahara. The teacher wearing his straw hat just stood there getting soaked with rain and laughing, a great belly laugh, "Ahaha. Hahaha." He had no desires, no thought for honor. That is best.

When I learned that Kenji often took his students off to Iwate Mountain or Taneyama gahara I wondered for a moment whether perhaps he had nothing better to do. After all, I can remember how hard my own parents worked following the war, raising five children, so busy that they did not know what time they got up or went to bed. I could not imagine any responsible adult going somewhere purely for idle pleasure. Even children like myself, we only went somewhere if it was a school excursion or similar event where someone else had made all the arrangements.

The lives of people in Iwate when Kenji was a teacher must have been at least as difficult as they were throughout Japan immediately after the war. Every adult must have had to work extremely hard. In such an environment then, what was Kenji's purpose in taking his students to Iwate Mountain or Taneyama gahara? I asked Neko, "What did you go there for?"

"We just went, that was all," he responded simply, but the very fact that they "just went" had remained in his heart.

They went and communed with nature in all its magnificence. At those times, they were able to assimilate Kenji's detachment from the ordinary world and feel the pulse of the universe. This experience stimulated that which lay deep inside each one of them, the heart of the universe, locked away and transcending their own desires; they were filled with the sheer bliss of being alive, the joy of existence itself. And from there, their beings could aim straight toward the essence of what made them human.

A Being in Harmony with Nature

Kenji often captured the things he did with his students in words as prose or poetry, which he called mental sketches, and read them aloud. In this way the students' own experiences became firmly rooted within them in the form of words, reinforcing the impact of the events upon them.

They themselves wrote and published the "Iwate Report,"

a record of the time they climbed Iwate Mountain. In this account, they have so assimilated Kenji's words and perceptions as to make the reader believe for a second that they are written by Kenji himself.

His students were completely captivated by their teacher. If he said, "Let's go!" they would follow unquestioningly without even asking their destination.

At 9:00 in the evening Kenji might unexpectedly appear and invite students in the dormitory to go out with him. They had not a clue where they were going and, following him, they might find themselves in Hanamaki or Ozawa hot springs. On the way, Kenji never walked in a straight line but rather would swim through the waving stalks of eulalia, or suddenly walk into the brush.

Once he stopped in the pitch dark and began conversing with someone despite the fact that no one was there. Unnerved, his students waited until he had finished talking and then asked, "Teacher, who were you talking to?"

"A one-eyed woman appeared and asked me if I really intended to persist," he replied.

At that time, cool weather had caused substantial crop failure and farming communities in Tohoku and Hokkaido were facing famine. The number of children suffering from malnutrition increased and some families were forced to sell their daughters. Kenji was deeply concerned by this and felt he must somehow rescue the farmers from their plight. The old woman, he said, had wanted to know whether his intention was sincere.

I think that Kenji was able to communicate with nature, that his being was receptive to the voices of such spirits in nature as the old woman. One of his students related that Kenji once said, "My thoughts have been transmitted to that forest over there, they are there now in the forest." I think that such communion with nature was indeed possible for him. The following poem, "The Forest Grove and My Thoughts," probably came into being after his conversation with this student.

Look! Do you see?
That small grove shaped like a mushroom
Wet with mist in the distance?
My thoughts flow so swiftly
Over there,
All of them,
Melting into it.
  This place is full of butterbur flowers.

The outer world that our eyes perceive, which attracts our hearts, is not just external but is also an expression of what lies within us. Likewise, Kenji's sketches of the external are, in themselves, an expression of his internal world.

To his students Kenji was certainly an "extraordinary" teacher. It was not just his unusual apparel, which consisted of spats over rubber-soled socks or round gumboots and overalls topped by a straw hat, but also his behavior that made him appear strange. He rarely walked normally, but would break into a run as they walked down the road, give a strange shout and leap into the air, or rustle through the weeds, and talk with invisible old women.

Far from being eccentric, however, this behavior was

perfectly normal; Kenji was simply being faithful to the feelings that sprang from within his being. Although some students may have had misgivings about their teacher, although they may have worried that his behavior could mean trouble, they were still won over by his natural charm.

The Truth Moves People's Hearts

"School was fun. He was really a fun teacher," Toshio Nagasaka says looking back on those days. Nagasaka is another with many memories of Kenji. One example is this story of a test of courage that Kenji organized.

Three of us were staying in the dormitory, taking our turn caring for the silkworms, when Mr. Miyazawa suddenly said, "Let's test your courage." He dared us to go and draw a circle with chalk on the big tombstone in the furthest corner of the graveyard. When we nervously tiptoed into the cemetery there was a sudden flash and a billow of white. Someone screamed "A ghost!" and we raced out of there . . . .

Scrambling back to the entrance of the dormitory, they found Kenji waiting. "What a bunch of cowards," he chided them. "You can't even go into a graveyard. I'm afraid none of you have passed the test." And he stomped off to his room, grumbling all the while. Later they learned that the flash of light had been caused by a light bulb, the kind used to decorate Christmas trees, while the white object was just a sheet. Kenji had carefully rigged it all ahead of time.

Early the next morning, he came to the dormitory. "What a miserable performance," he announced. "You all failed last night's test. I cannot pass even one of you. Today, for sure, I want you to succeed." This time he dared them to jump off the roof of the silkworm shed, a two-story building.

Fortunately, the ground beneath was the soft soil of a field, so Nagasaka and the others were able to muster the courage to jump.

"Well done! You have all passed," Kenji praised them. He was reportedly very pleased and returned to his quarters in an excellent humor.

In all likelihood Kenji was putting on an act. It must have been hard to suppress his mirth at the sight of their discomfiture when he told them to jump off the roof. Unaware that Kenji's laments over their cowardice were a pretense, all of his students leapt from the roof in their desire to live up to his expectations. Kenji was greatly pleased with this, enjoying his little joke immensely.

Many of the things his students remember him doing would be impermissible in the schools of today. Someone could break a bone jumping from the roof of a two-story silkworm shed. If a teacher took his students to Taneyama gahara with its fierce thunderstorms, someone might be struck and killed by lightning.

Once Kenji took his students out late at night to hike in the mountains. In mid-hike, one of his students became so exhausted that he "flopped onto the ground like a cow patty" and fell fast asleep, staying there until morning. The other students, continuing on, found that their destination was a hot-spring area. They had not brought any money, however, and instead left promissory notes to send money later as they made the rounds of the baths.

Another time, Kenji took his students across a railroad bridge. The Kitagami River rushed beneath it and they were so terrified that they cowered in fright when they reached the middle.

Schools today would never allow a teacher to do such things, and teachers themselves would not even consider it. But it is these types of experiences that spark a major happening within a student's being. Even those students who followed Kenji reluctantly, who found it hard to adjust to his ways, must have experienced some kind of happening.

When people are exposed to truthful actions or sincere words, it sparks something within them. Having experienced the quality of Kenji's classes, Neko said, "Honesty, sincerity, truth move people's hearts," and that very sincerity had a major impact on each of his students, remaining with them in later years. Going to Taneyama gahara, climbing Iwate Mountain, touring the hot springs, all of these were acts of simple, unadorned sincerity.

The addition of a new section to the school generated a great deal of rubble which was piled in a corner of the school ground. Kenji's students danced with abandon on top of this in time to records that Kenji played. It was so much fun, it left an indelible impression on them. This is honesty; this is a genuine lesson.

Lessons are perceived as having specific objectives, consciously planned to convey content in a specific way. However, this kind of teaching does not reach students.

Only that which springs unconsciously from one's being can be effectively transmitted to others.

As Kenji wrote in his book *Nomingeijutsu gairon koyo* (An Introduction to Peasant Art), "That which does not spring from the subconscious is impotent or a sham." It is the subconscious things from within one's being rather than the intent to educate in a specific way that really communicate, and anything else is "impotent or a sham."

Kenji always acted or expressed himself in honest obedience to the inspirations of his subconscious, those things that welled up naturally from his being. That is why it is essential to understand the type of being he possessed when discussing him.

Clear Channels

There are several perspectives that provide clues to understanding Kenji's being. One of these is his approach to Western music.

At that time, I believe few Japanese felt any affinity for Western music. Accustomed to music that used gongs, drums, free-reed mouth organs, and the flageolet-type instruments of Shinto ceremonies, the honest reaction of most Japanese when they first heard classical music must have been complete bewilderment.

Kenji often invited his students to his home and played records of Western music for them. When they had finished listening he served them snacks. The students themselves came for the food, and would wait expectantly, hoping that he would turn the record off soon. But while the music was playing, Kenji's mind would fill with one image after another, and he would make such remarks as "the feather on the lady's hat is stirred by the breeze," "a shaft of moonlight pierces the darkness," "snow is falling," "can't you hear the sounds of the waves," or "the wind has begun to blow."

Kenji felt the music with his entire being and it inspired countless images. Such a response to classical music was very rare for a Japanese person of that time. What made his being so different from that of his contemporaries?

In my own case, the first music that powerfully affected me was Dvořák's *From the New World*. This symphony permeated my entire being without the least resistance. Therefore it was difficult for me to understand people who felt no affinity for it, who could not understand what it was about. It was not until I studied at the Takeuchi Drama Research Center, which was implementing such original programs as "Body and Word Lessons," that I realized how greatly people's responsiveness varies.

For example, one lesson consists of moving your body in pursuit of the images you receive while listening to music. When Stravinsky's *The Rite of Spring* begins to play, even if you have never heard the title, that world appears before you and you begin to move and dance, becoming various living creatures. In other lessons, you listen to a single word and pursue the image it invokes. However, there were some among us for whom music and words evoked no images at all.

In a lesson on words, the moment Mr. Takeuchi said "valley" I had an image of myself crawling desperately up a rugged cliff with my feet slipping out from under me, and I pursued that image, but one of our members could only conjure up the Chinese character for "valley." No visual image came to him at all. I was stunned and profoundly impressed by the fact that for some, images do not simply well forth naturally from their being.

I also experienced a change in my response to the Beatles' music, which until I attended the Takeuchi Drama Research Center I had thought to be noisy. With the development of a more sensitive being and through *seitai* exercises developed by Dr. Haruya Noguchi, which utilize the body's natural energy or *ki* and are applicable in daily life, I was able to dissolve inner tensions and facilitate a reconnection to the whole. As a consequence, the Beatles' music became easy listening. Through education, my being itself had changed.

Perhaps the ability to listen atrophies when one's being becomes stiff and rigid, restricting the flow of images. We have countless senses for feeling things, but the environment in which a person is raised and the customs within which he or she lives can restrict the number of senses that are able to function.

During a lecture at the Asahi Culture Center, the sociologist Sosuke Mita related a story which amply illustrates this point. A Westerner made a movie to enlighten some African people. When he showed it to them and asked for their impressions, however, he found that his message had not gotten through at all. The only scene the audience remembered was one in which a chicken ran across the set. The director had no recollection of even shooting such a scene. Rewinding the film, he found that a chicken had indeed run across the screen once for a single brief moment during the entire movie.

In other words, our perceptions are limited to those senses for which the channels are open, and we cannot receive anything via senses for which the channels are closed. That is the way our beings are made.

In this context, we can say that Kenji's being, with its ability to respond to Western music and communicate with spirits, was slightly different from that of the average Japanese of his generation, for many of his senses were clear, open channels that allowed a fresh breeze to flow through.

A Being Faithful to the Spirit

One of the factors that allowed Kenji to develop such open sensitivity was the home environment in which he was born and raised.

He often read what he wrote to his younger brother, Seiroku, and to his sisters and listened to their reactions. In the Japan of the early 1900s, however, such frank give and take within a family was unusual. In his middle school years, he taught his siblings to sing poems by Tsuchi Bansui which he had learned at school, and they sang them together, which makes one think of the type of open family communication found in modern homes.

The fact that his younger sister Toshi became a schoolteacher and lived independently after graduating from Japan Women's University was also very unusual even in a major city within a rural area. His mother, Ichi, herself, seems to have shed the old ways of thinking which dictated that women should marry and obey their husbands.

Of course, as is frequently mentioned, Kenji had fierce confrontations with his father, Seijiro, concerning their religious beliefs. They argued so heatedly that his younger sisters worried whether such angry debate was appropriate between father and son. Kenji also rebelled against the family business, which he despised, and against certain attitudes of his father's.

The following is a famous tanka he wrote concerning the day he entered middle school:

Father, oh, father. Why wind your great silver watch in front of the
   housemaster?

Kenji's father, accompanying him to the entrance ceremony, had ostentatiously produced his silver pocket watch in front of the dormitory superintendent and wound it in a deliberate display. Kenji was mortified by his father's attachment to riches, by his material desires. This tanka vents his disgust for his father's actions, demanding to know how he could stoop so low. It was one way of expressing his rebellion against his father's snobbery.

He also argued vehemently with his father concerning religious beliefs. There is no doubt that such occurrences indicate genuine conflict between Kenji and his father, a conflict that cast a dark shadow over their home. But this does not mean that their conflict had only a negative effect on the family. Rather, it indicates that within Kenji's family there existed a certain amount of freedom to challenge and criticize the father's views.

More important here is the fact that Kenji, who was raised in such a home environment, did not boast to others, saying, "Hey, look at my father's watch. Impressive, isn't it?" when his father strutted. Rather, his being caused him to feel the exact opposite, and gave him the strength of will to express what he felt.

Born the eldest son of a prominent and wealthy merchant in the Hanamaki area who ran a pawnshop and secondhand clothing store, Kenji was naturally expected to inherit and run the business. However, he deplored the fact that it preyed upon the suffering of the socially and economically disadvantaged. So, while on the one hand he did not lack filial gratitude, at the same time, he obdurately refused to succeed to his father's business. Kenji's feelings did not soften despite his father's repeated remonstrations. His sense of shame concerning his father's flaunting of his material possessions, such as his display of the pocket watch, and his aversion to the family business basically arose from the same sentiment. He felt extremely guilty for possessing material wealth in the midst of, or rather due to the existence of, the poverty of those around him.

According to one well-known anecdote, Kenji once burst into tears when he came in contact with the lives of the clients forced to pawn their goods, exclaiming, "The world is unfair. I hate this business which profits from other people's troubles." In another famous incident, Kenji's father scolded him for lending a client the sum he asked without even inquiring into the value of the goods he had brought. "If you lend more than their value for such worthless goods, we'll go bankrupt," he argued, but Kenji insisted that "That is what the man said he needed."

For Kenji, who lived in accordance with the spirit of heaven, the logic of owning money simply did not agree with his being. In the poem "*Kokubetsu*" (Valediction), he writes "Not even man belongs to man." How much less so, then, can money be considered the property of man.

When Kenji was not true to his own being, his health quickly deteriorated. When he was preparing to graduate from middle school, his father refused to allow him to continue his studies at Morioka Agricultural College because he felt that Kenji needed no further education to run the pawnshop. Immediately after this announcement, Kenji's grades dropped drastically, and in the end he graduated with lower than average grades. That was not all. At the time of graduation, he had to undergo an operation for hypertrophic rhinitis, developed a high fever, and was hospitalized for suspected typhus. After being discharged, he suffered from neurosis which sapped any energy he might have devoted to his duties in the store. Seeing this, his parents finally accepted the fact that commerce did not suit his character. They relented and gave him permission to continue his studies, whereupon he immersed himself in studying for the entrance exams, entering the agriculture department of Morioka Agricultural College as a scholarship student.

In this way, Kenji's spirit was faithfully manifested in his physical being. He possessed the capacity to feel a tremendous range of feelings and honestly expressed everything that he felt. That was the type of being he was.

The Pros and Cons of Prosperity

From another perspective, the fact that Kenji became physically ill in the face of his parents' opposition to further education indicates that his economic situation allowed him the luxury of illness. In an ordinary household of that time, someone who graduated from middle school would have tried his best to become financially independent, starting work as soon as possible so that he could send some money to his parents and thereby ease their hardship, however slightly. Children of destitute families did not have time to be sick.

When I was attending classes at the main branch of the Noguchi Seitai School, I heard a convincing lecture by Haruya Noguchi's son Hiroyuki, who said that the best way to swiftly detach children from material desires is to give them more material things than they could ever want, approaching the task with the attitude that it does not matter if you expend all of your family's material resources, pressing them with goods and urging them on, saying, "Oh, here, let me buy this, too. Surely you want it." As I listened to him explain that in this way children will learn at an early age that truly important things are not material, freeing them from material desires, I thought of Kenji.

A degree of economic leeway puts one in a position to view the whole. Without it, one must struggle just to put food on the table, and each day is focussed on basic material survival. Financial security is what allows one to see the whole, to develop a world view and a systematic philosophy, to turn one's gaze to the universe.

His family's economic prosperity was certainly a major factor in Kenji's life in many ways. From early on, he was aware that there was something important in this world that transcended money, which is why he never became attached to material things. A teacher who lived in the same dormitory with Kenji testifies to the fact that he had absolutely no material desires, but doubtlessly one of the reasons he could be so detached was the very fact that he came from a wealthy family.

It is true that Kenji felt guilty about his family's wealth, that he felt their money was defiled because it was obtained from the impoverished, and that in his anguish at his predicament he insisted that in his next life he did not want to be born to riches. However, it must be acknowledged that his family's wealth also had some positive influence.

All Things Are Connected

Of course, his family's wealth was not the only decisive influence on the formation of Kenji's worldview. Wealth was the economic environmental factor that shaped his perspective, but it was the spirit of Buddhism that imparted real power to him, and I believe its influence was substantial.

For example, in the Diamond Sutra, living creatures are defined as follows:

"In nirvana, all creatures, whether born from eggs or from wombs, from moisture or by transformation, colored or colorless, thinking or non-thinking, are annihilated in order to be saved."

The worldview that maintains that all things in the universe, those with form and those without, are united in a single whole is found here. When Kenji declares in *An Introduction to Peasant Art* that "the happiness of the individual cannot be attained without first realizing the happiness of the whole world," the expression "the whole world" does not refer solely to the world of man but embraces all created things in the entire universe. This view is, in essence, the same as that expressed in the Diamond Sutra.

I do not mean to claim that Kenji came to hold this world view from reading the Diamond Sutra. Rather, the Diamond Sutra touched something within Kenji that he had already intuited from nature, and therefore he accepted it, recognizing it as something that he had felt all along. Perhaps one could say that Kenji's very being, with its capacity to intuit such things and his eager longing, attracted the truth from science and religion and through exposure to these truths, his own worldview took shape.

Insects, plants, and minerals, light, clouds, rain, and wind all appear in his works. And they speak with men and animals. This is not mere personification. To him, all of these things were in reality himself, and he in turn was them.

I believe that from an early age Kenji was attuned to the fact that all things in the universe, whether animate or inanimate, are one.

For example he concludes the poem *"Taneyama to Taneyama gahara Pahto III"* (Taneyama and Taneyama gahara, Part III) as follows:

Mountain ridges rolling in countless layers, like waves on the sea,
And the gentle, gentle swelling and falling line of heaven's end.
Ah, all things, everything is crystal clear.
When a cloud is formed by wind and water, air and light and
   particles of dust,
Wind, water, the lithosphere, myself, too, are all equal part of that
   composition.
I am, in reality, but one drop of water, of the wind,
And the fact that I know this
Is because the water, the light, the wind, are me.
...Those mountain ridges, each one is a small organ...

Kenji did not perceive nature as mere scenery to be viewed, but rather felt that nature in its entirety was himself. His being was endowed with this type of receptivity.

Let us look at a poem he wrote from his sickbed when he was thirty-three, four years before his death.

I will die soon,
Today or perhaps tomorrow.
I ponder anew what I am,
In the end, I am nothing but the Law.
My body, my bones, my blood, my flesh
Are but myriad molecules,
The union of various atoms
And those atoms are finally but a single void.
And the external world, also.
That is how I see myself and the external world.

And the law which operates upon these sundry materials
I call my self.
Whether I die and return to the void,
Or whether I feel my self once again,
Only one Law operates here.
This original Law has been called the Lotus Sutra.
Because their hearts seek the way, people believe in bodhisattva,
Through belief in bodhisattva, they believe in Buddha,
And the countless Buddhas, too, are the Law,
And the original Law of the many Buddhas is the Lotus Sutra.
I will obey the Lotus Sutra of the Supreme Law.
To live is the Supreme Law,
To die is the Supreme Law,
From now unto eternity, I hold fast to the Law.

Ultimately all things in the universe are joined together. Animate and inanimate, all exist within the will of the macrocosm, and through the movement of that will are born and extinguished. That is the law of the universe. Life and death, too, all obey the law of the universe. Within that context all things are equal. Kenji was firmly convinced of this.

In the midst of a society where the one thing people can tolerate is other people's pain, Kenji's sensitivity to the suffering of others sprang from this viewpoint. Or perhaps it would be more appropriate to say that it sprang from his being which made him responsive to this type of world view.

After his younger sister Toshi's death, Kenji traveled north in search of her soul. In a verse of the poem "*Aomori banka*" (Aomori Elegy) which reads

> We are all, from of old, brothers and sisters,
> So one should not pray for only one soul,
> Ah, this I did not do.

one can glimpse the almost frightening gravity of the deep connection of all existing things in this world, and Kenji's profound respect for the stern fact that "all living things have been in perpetual motion, from long ages past."

Lending people as much money as they asked for in exchange for the goods they brought to pawn was, for Kenji, completely natural behavior. To those in need, he gave without restraint. For this reason, he ran out of money when he was a student at Morioka Agricultural College and had to walk about 40 kilometers from Morioka to Hanamaki. Similarly, as a teacher at the Agricultural School he gave the greater part of his salary to a colleague who was hospitalized. That was the type of being he was.

Confronting His Life Earnestly

The greatest influence on Kenji's self-development was his father.

As mentioned before, in mid-adolescence he and his father, Seijiro, began to have fierce arguments about whether he would inherit the business and about religious issues. Kenji insisted that he did not care where he lived, as long as he did not have to live at home, that he did not care what occupation he undertook, as long as it was not the family business. His father, in turn, remonstrated with him.

But no matter how he lectured, Kenji refuted his reasons and their confrontations became increasingly heated. His younger sister Shige recalls, "My brother and father argued about issues that went right to the roots of human life, my brother attacking the impotence of my father's Jodoshinshu beliefs and rejecting his material success, his status, and his possessions. They argued so violently day after day that my mother and all of us were concerned. I wondered whether other fathers ever fought with their sons like this."

In 1918, still only twenty-two years of age, Kenji, perhaps because he could no longer bear these confrontations with his father, frequently intimated to others that he planned to leave home or go abroad. His father when he learned of this was consumed with a blazing rage that did not abate for several days.

Kenji wrote to his friend Kanai Hosaka in a letter dated August 1919 as follows:

Recently my father tells me daily, "You graduated from agricultural college when the rest of the world is suffering and yet you behave miserably. Think! Be of some use to others. You're outrageous! Dabbling in woodblock prints!

And to even consider jaunting off to America is disgraceful.

You have forgotten the first duty of life. You have strayed from the right path."...And stray I will. Just watch this heretical wanderer. Everything I learned at school is rubbish.

The intensity of their debate can be gleaned from this letter. His father's remark concerning woodblock prints refers to Kenji's large collection of prints.

I would like to introduce one further example, part of a letter Kenji wrote to his father immediately prior to graduating from Morioka Agricultural College.

Perhaps through lack of sufficient faith, I frequently disobey you, Father, and I am truly sorry for it. Which is why it has been constantly on my mind since I returned to Morioka. I have caused you considerable concern, being twice afflicted with illnesses that brought me to death's door, once with a contagious disease. And not only that, but I transmitted the latter to you so that your intestine is still affected. You have granted my desire to enter college in this time when such schooling is a luxury, and given me books of which other students can only dream. Yet, through some quirk of malcontent, I contradict your will. If our beliefs differ, I should simply resign myself and weep, but instead I am so bold as to become angry with you. It must be our karma determined by a previous life. Whatever the reason, when I come near you, I am filled only with rebellion. Then, after returning to Morioka, to my great shame, I disobey you once again and am filled with remorse.

Kenji has no choice but to follow the path of his beliefs. And he is begging his father to give him his blessing. In the same letter, Kenji writes, "If to fulfill one's filial duty in this world truly means to work hard, build an impressive home, leave noble offspring to the world, and ensure that they suffer no privation, can one really attain true satisfaction through this?"

Even Kenji can understand the desire to acquire what happiness the world has to offer, to please one's parents. But he must declare with mixed feelings, torn as he is between his love for his parents and his own beliefs, that this kind of life is impossible for him.

The conflict between father and son continued until just prior to Kenji's death at the age of thirty-seven. As he approached his final hour, his father finally acknowledged him, saying, "You, too, are a great man." Kenji, looking very pleased, declared, "I have finally been praised by my own father" and drew his last breath.

How did he come to have this strong desire for self-determination that enabled him to live in accordance with his beliefs without being caught up in wordly pursuits? This is an extremely intriguing point. Let us look at the first half of his poem "*Haru to Ashura*" (Spring and the Ashura).

From the gray steel of images
Akebia vines coil round a spider,
Covering the rose thicket,
The marshy ground in a twisted pattern of adulation.
(Fragments of amber pour down
thicker than woodwinds at noon)
The bitterness, the blueness of anger
I am an Ashura
Spitting, gnashing my teeth, pacing to and fro
Beneath the shining layers of April air.

(The scene is distorted by tears)
Tattered clouds limit my vision
A clear crystal wind traverses
The translucent sea of heaven
Zypressen – a row of spring
In deep black, drink ether–
Despite the sharpness of snow on heaven's mount
Which shines even from their dark trunks,
(Shimmering heat waves and polarized light)
The words of truth have been lost
Clouds shred and fly across the sky
Ah, at the depths of a radiant April
Gnashing my teeth, burning, pacing to and fro
I am an Ashura.

The "twisted pattern of adulation" mentioned at the beginning of the poem represents Kenji's inner self, the Ashura who, unable to be perfect, is torn by various inner contradictions. The "zypressen," or cypress, represent that part of him that rejects the twisted, damp, and soiled self and seeks to rise above it, striving toward the heavens. It is a symbol of Kenji's own yearning and endeavors toward self-development blazing straight up from the swampy ground with its agonizing tangle of adulation and flattery.

And the fire of Kenji's longing, his striving for self-determination could not have burned so fiercely without the presence of his father, Seijiro. Their fierce arguments only served to intensify Kenji's beliefs, and I doubt that the cypress and all it represents would have been born with such heat and intensity within him if his father had simply accepted him as he was and never tried to divert him from his chosen path.

Most of Kenji's criticisms of his father were directed at Jodoshinshu, a Buddhist sect of which his father was a strong adherent. Kenji accused Jodoshinshu of having degenerated into a profit-oriented business, making its adherents feel grateful while in reality mercilessly exploiting them.

In the tale "*Kumo, Namekuji, to Tanuki*" (The Spider, the Slug, and the Raccoon), a rabbit allows itself to be devoured by a raccoon, convinced by the latter that it should be grateful for this bounty bestowed upon it by the great goddess, Wildcat. Kenji obviously wrote this work with the Jodoshinshu sect in mind, and as such, it may be said to be the product of his conflict with his father.

Kenji's younger brother, Seiroku, relates in his memoirs that when Kenji read this story to him and his younger sisters, they howled with laughter, holding themselves around the middle and rolling about the floor. They understood his implied meaning only too well.

Kenji did not compromise with his father. Most people's approach to success in life is to accept things as they are and to make compromises accordingly, but for Kenji this was impossible because the clashes between the two of them were for him a matter of extreme gravity, even of life and death.

To accept or not to accept compromise was a crucial issue that concerned his entire being. Any compromise at such a point would mean a life no better than death.

The very fact that his self-determination was firmly rooted

rather than superficial meant that he must do what he said. He needed that amount of resolution to stand up to his father.

And because he was Kenji, he did not bend under scathing criticisms from his father such as, "Do you really imagine that such gibberish will sell? Why don't you go to a bookstore and see what's selling these days?"

How many people at that time could understand Kenji? A teacher at the same dormitory testifies that "Mr. Miyazawa did not have any friends." But Kenji did not live his life in consideration of whether people understood him or not. He lived in another dimension, in a world where life was in deadly earnest. Because the most important thing to Kenji was to confront life honestly, to fulfill his destiny.

Living in Accord with What His Being Felt

Kenji needed the philosophies of both the Orient and the Occident to develop his personal worldview and his own self. He searched avidly through countless volumes, particularly foreign books that concentrated on Europe. One of his students, Rokuro Asakura, remembers that "our teacher was always reading books in foreign languages. In the afternoon when our lessons were finished he would sit on the riverbank or in the school grounds which were covered in clover and read foreign books in their original language. And the book he was reading changed from day to day." He obviously read much more than the average person. And it is certain that portions of the books he read gave words to the things he felt within, providing hints for giving form to his thoughts. He excelled at languages, and is said to have mastered not only English but German, Italian, and Russian, among others, but he mastered them in response to a specific need within his being.

Kenji strove to be loyal to what he felt. It never occurred to him to betray that in order to be understood by others. It did not matter to him whether he was alone or not, for he, who was at one with nature, was probably never truly alone. I do not think that he was so sentimental as to feel alone or lonely because others did not understand him. And I think that the reason he did not need others was because he had received sufficient love in his childhood. People who have been loved enough do not worry about whether others understand them, nor do they adapt themselves to others in order to be understood. Instead they can devote themselves to attaining what they want.

Kenji published only two works while he was alive, *Spring and the Ashura*, a collection of poetry, and *Chumon no Oi Resutoran* (A Restaurant of Many Orders), a collection of stories. Neither of them received wide acclaim. *Spring and the Ashura* was marked down in price because it did not sell, while *A Restaurant of Many Orders* was mistaken for a cookbook and placed in the wrong section of the bookstore. Moreover, both were published at the author's expense and he received no royalties. The only income Kenji earned from writing while he was alive was reportedly from publication of a story "*Yuki Watari*" (Snow Crossing) in the magazine *Aikoku Fujin* (Patriotic Women).

In the face of this situation, one would expect him to at least compromise temporarily and write something easier to read, something that would sell, but for Kenji this was impossible. He had no choice but to express honestly and to the very best of his ability what he felt with his being, what rose from the depths of his heart.

He was capable of this because he believed in the reader's pure essence. It was thus only natural for him to express what he felt as he felt it without any compromise. Even in the case of *An Introduction to Peasant Art*, he was surely aware that some people would at first find it impossible to understand. But, despite this, he still expressed his thoughts truly and accurately in a form with which he himself could be satisfied, for peasants, and for himself.

In the above-mentioned work, he writes:

> To live strongly and truly is to live in awareness of the galaxy within you and to respond to it.
>
> Let us seek true happiness for the whole world; the search itself is the path.

It is the awareness that the galactic system is part of one's own self that is important. The entire universe, all created things including ourselves are united in a single whole. Our own existence is but an expression of the will of the universe; the plants, the trees, all things exist as an expression of this will. Accordingly, because we are all interconnected, "the happiness of the individual cannot be attained without first realizing the happiness of the whole world." Not just for the Japanese but for all the peoples of the world. Not just for human beings but for all beings that exist on this planet, in this universe. If the welfare of all is not assured, then there can be no happiness for humankind. A glance at even one of the many environmental issues facing us today makes this clear. Where the welfare of plants and animals is abused, the welfare of humankind is unattainable. Environmental destruction leads to the extermination of the entire human race. As long as each individual remains unaware of this fact, true happiness cannot be attained. Kenji's being was like a filter, which sifted his actions to determine whether they were in tune with the laws of the galaxy. He could feel the universe, and what was happiness within it.

There are probably many people who are under the impression that Kenji's life was an unhappy one, a life of self-abnegation. Personally, I do not think so. Kenji was a happy man who had the luxury of living his life in the way he chose, of living in accordance with the laws of heaven.

Expressing What He Received from Nature

The foreword to Kenji's collection of tales *A Restaurant of Many Orders* gives us a good idea of how he responded to nature as an expression of the will of the universe, and of what he felt from nature. His explanation is easy to understand.

Although we may never get as much sugar candy as we want, we can always taste the clear, transparent wind and drink the beautiful peach-colored light at sunrise.

And many times I have seen the raggedest clothes transformed in field and forest into the most exquisite velvet, woolen, or jeweled finery.

I prefer such splendid food and apparel.

All of the stories in this book were given to me by the rainbow or the moonlight, in the forests, the meadows, or along the railroad tracks.

When I walk alone past the blue twilight of the oak wood or stand shivering in the midst of a November wind on the mountain, I just cannot help but feel that these things are real. Truly, I simply cannot help but believe that this is what actually happened, and write it down just as it is.

And so, within these stories there may be some things that are for you. And then again, there may be some things that are not. But I cannot tell the two apart. There may be places where you wonder what on earth I am talking about, and in truth, I do not even know myself.

However, you will never know how much I long for even a small fragment of these little stories to become in the end crystal-clear, true nourishment for you.

Kenji wrote these tales just as he received them or felt them from the rainbow or the moonlight as he walked in the woods, the meadows, or along the railroad tracks. In that sense, they are not allegorical. His being was actually capable of receiving many things from nature and his stories are in the end the truth that he saw, heard, narrated, and felt with his entire being.

When he gazed upon a flower, he could hear each word it spoke. Having had a similar experience myself, I can understand this very well.

In his story *"Wakai Kodama"* (The Young Dryad), he writes about dogtooth violets rejoicing at the coming of spring.

The hollow was covered in plump moss, and here and there gentle dogtooth violets bloomed. The dryad could not clearly see their superb pale purple flowers because they fluttered indistinctly and unsteadily in the breeze.

Rather he read the uncertain purple letters which appeared one after the other above the glossy green leaves only to disappear again.

"It's spring! It's spring! Spring has come!" Each letter came to life one by one, drew breath, disappeared, then reappeared only to vanish once more.

This is how Kenji actually perceived the leaves of the dogtooth violet shimmering in the spring sunlight. Similarly, in his work, *"Okinagusa"* (The Pasque-Flowers) two pasque-flowers converse.

"Look! The cloud is going to cover the sun again. See, that field over there is already in shadow."

"It's speeding this way. How fast it is! The larch trees are already darkened; now it's gone."

Kenji actually heard this conversation "quieter than a dream." He did not make the animals, the plants, or trees speak because it was a children's story, but because as he himself wrote, "I simply cannot help but believe that this is what actually happened, and write it down just as it is." He wrote it as he experienced it because his being was capable of experiencing it in that way.

Kenji described the difference between poetry and mental sketches to his student Soroku Suzuki, who graduated from Hanamaki Agricultural School in 1923. Although not an exact quotation, the gist of his description may be paraphrased as follows:

> The words I have now are out of synch with tanka. On that point, verse is well suited to the words I possess and expresses them truthfully. However, the things that I write, although they may follow the form of poetry are not poems but mental sketches. If people want to call them poems, it does not matter, but I am doing the same thing with words that a painter does when he transfers a scene onto canvas. It is different from personification, or borrowing phenomena by saying "it is as something as a something" or "it is just like a something," because I am expressing phenomena as they really are. This makes a deeper impression and evokes sympathy. And through this a transformation will surely occur in the boundaries of composition.

In other words, for Kenji, phenomena as they existed in nature were the scenery of his soul. For example, when he wrote "the ibis fire of the vivid dawn" he was not saying that the eastern sky at dawn blazed like an ibis. Rather, it was an ibis fire; that was his mental image.

He had the same sensitivity as a musician who reproduces wind and light through sounds. His being was an open channel capable of feeling such things.

Kunio Oda, another of Kenji's students, told me that when walking together, his teacher would make remarks that were incomprehensible to others, such as, "The spirits of the trees are talking" or "My thoughts have moved into that tree" or "People are a part of nature, too." Kenji had the power to hear the inaudible and see the invisible.

And precisely because he had that power he was able to record his mental images of phenomena in the outer world.

The famous poet Shinpei Kusano comments on Kenji's method of poetry composition as follows:

> The methods of "recording" or "sketching" brought results that exceeded the limits of conventional poetic composition. Kenji walked the fields and mountains with a mechanical pencil hanging from a string around his neck. The majority of poems he wrote before becoming confined to his sickbed were written in the open air. He sketched by the light of the campfire, in the train as he journeyed, or at times, while he walked...
>
> Kenji's eyes were a 16mm projector, and writing cranked the projector's handle.

I, too, believe this. Kenji's goal was to record the outer world exactly as he saw and felt it, and this became a concise record of the mental scenery within himself.

In a letter dated February 9, 1925, to Saichi Mori, a famous writer who went by the pen name of Soichi Mori, Kenji wrote:

Spring and the Ashura which I published at my own expense, and every other work I have written to date, come nowhere near poetry. They are merely simple sketches of mental images jotted down under various conditions whenever circumstances permit, because proper study is impossible at this time, in preparation for the psychological work which I wish to complete in the future.

If these were mental sketches jotted down in preparation for his future work, then it mattered not at all if they were beyond the comprehension of his readers. There was no special need to write with any expectation that the reader would understand. This view is supported by Kenji's remarks addressed in a letter to his friend Hikaru Hahaki, dated June 19, 1932. "In no way am I writing these mental sketches in this day and age to appeal to the masses."

He is reported to have frequently stated to Yoshihide Shirafuji, who lived in the same dormitory, that "poetry and songs should be written in one's youth when creativity flourishes because as one grows older one's inspiration dries up and lacks vitality. One does not need to sacrifice one's own principles for those of society in order to create a great work. Therefore I do not concern myself with how others will appraise my poems." Kenji felt that eventually people would come to understand his writings and therefore he should express what he felt honestly without catering to the "real" world. After all, even if nobody ever understood his work, what did it matter?

Unfettered Freedom

Just as a musician transposes light or wind, which he experiences with his entire being, into sound, so Kenji transposed them into letters. It is very rare for a Japanese to possess a being so open to experiencing the external world, and in that sense, he was atypical.

If we think of dance, some, like European ballet, use movements that aspire heavenward, such as standing on tiptoe. In most Japanese folk dances, however, the dancers stamp the earth with their feet.

Even in terms of body movement, Kenji was not typically Japanese for whenever he was moved by a sound or a discovery in nature, he would emit a strange cry and dance in the air, a fact frequently mentioned by his students. He was much more capable than his fellow Japanese of experiencing the physical sensation of lightness, of shedding his material heaviness to soar effortlessly in space.

The ability to feel light and agile requires that one cast aside any bonds or restrictions. Like all of us, Kenji was bound by many fetters including the issue of his succession to the family business and the conflict between his father and himself. Yet I think that he strove to avoid creating unnecessary restrictions in his relationships with others, that he tried in his daily life to free himself from such fetters.

In the story "*Kaeru no gomugutsu*" (The Frog's Rubber Boots) he describes the lack of freedom resulting from relationships. Three frogs, Kan, Bun, and Ben, have the following conversation.

56

"Rubber boots are very popular among the Helon these days." [Helon is a Frogish term for human beings.]

"Yes. Everyone seems to be wearing them."

"We'd like some ourselves, wouldn't we?"

Kan wants rubber boots so desperately that he goes to the field mouse and begs him to get some. The field mouse readily consents, saying, "How could I possibly forget your kindness to me last year when you nursed me after I ate that buckwheat dumpling, was stricken with typhus, and became deathly ill." The next night, however, when he gives Kan his boots, he is in a foul humor and stomps off in a huff, saying, "You have no idea how difficult it was. It was very troublesome. In fact, I risked my life. I have hereby repaid my debt. I may even have paid a little too much."

At first, Kan wonders why the field mouse is so upset, but when he thinks about it, he realizes that it is perfectly understandable. First, the field mouse asked a rat. The rat asked a cat, the cat asked a dog, and the dog asked a horse. The horse managed to hoodwink his master to obtain a pair of rubber boots. These he gave to the dog, who gave them to the cat, who gave them to the rat, who gave them to the field mouse. But none of them handed the boots over wordlessly. With each exchange, the boots were accompanied by a demand for compensation or some other upsetting remark. And the horse would be in trouble if his deception was discovered by his master. The field mouse had to worry about all of these things, and thus the task had no doubt caused him a great deal of bother, even endangering his life.

57

Kenji's ability to write such a story illustrates his keen insight into the world around him. Many people increase the fetters that bind them by requesting things of others and by accepting requests with the expectation of receiving something in return. Kenji was a shrewd observer of this aspect of society.

Most probably, he himself hated to feel or to make others feel the confinement of such obligations, the curtailment of freedom that such fetters induce. According to the testimony of his students, he never accepted compensation for his services. Even if, for example, he planned a farmer's fertilizer schedule, he absolutely refused any payment. His skills were not on loan to others, and therefore, were free. He did not expect anything in return for service or gifts. It never occurred to him to harbor the slightest expectation of return because nothing, neither money nor material things, belongs to oneself. It is only natural therefore to share these things with others.

Kenji believed, above all, that everything in the universe circulated, that nothing belonged to him or was his to keep. As he states in the poem "*Kokubetsu*" (Valediction), "even man does not belong to man." Ultimately, then, how much less do money or material things belong to any one person.

Artists generally have tended to be less hampered by social or material conventions. This may be due in part to the fact that such work does not generate much income. It meant, however, that people like Mozart, van Gogh, and Kenji were much freer. In later years, many people made a living by exploiting Mozart, van Gogh, or Kenji, but none of the latter ever encumbered themselves with material wealth and so they must have been extremely light of spirit.

What Kenji Gained from the Mountains

When thinking about Kenji, we must give serious attention to why he so often visited Taneyama gahara or Iwate Mountain.

Even he must have tired of many aspects involved in living in this temporal, material world. In his poem "*Seito shokun ni yoseru*" (To My Students) which he wrote when he resigned from his job at Hanamaki Agricultural School, he states,

These four years
    What joy they brought me.
Every day
    I sang like a bird in the classroom.
I swear
    That in this work
I never remember being tired.

The statement "in this work, I never remember being tired" implies that outside his work in the classroom, there were things that tired him; that he found some work that did not involve direct contact with his students exhausting.

The mountains were the sacred ground of Kenji's soul. When his spirit drooped, surely he went to the mountains to receive their sacred energy. To receive such energy, one must open the channels of sensitivity which become clogged by daily living, and for Kenji, Taneyama gahara and Iwate Mountain were places that cleared the passageways for the universal creativity that welled within his being.

When exhaustion is so complete that we come to despise everything, the channel of creativity is obstructed and we feel nothing, not even if someone is standing right beside us. Parents, for example, can become so blocked when they are preoccupied with worry that they do not even have eyes for their own children.

But if some chance encounter opens the channel, the outer world comes flooding in. By going to the mountains, Kenji opened wide the door leading to the sublime, conversing with nature and simply absorbing its spirit. When someone chances upon a scene of breathtaking beauty, he can be so overcome by ecstasy that he feels content to die right then and there, and certainly Kenji tasted this same sense of bliss in the mountains. He did not go to the mountains because he happened to have spare time, but because the mountains and plateaus were essential for replenishing and sustaining his true self. They gave him a creative power that never ran dry.

In the mountains he saw stars scattered across the universe or clouds racing over the vast sky, a small wild grape, pasque-flowers or ants at his feet. When he visited the mountains, his perception expanded, roving freely from high in the universe and the sky down to his feet, and from his feet to the spreading meadows. His eyes, which, to borrow Shinpei Kusano's words, became "a 16mm projector," could simultaneously capture countless layers of life.

His gaze was not only focused from the earth heavenward.

At times, his being floated in the heavens and his perspective was directed from the heavens earthward.

For example, he frequently used the phrase "heaven's end" to describe the horizon, as in the poem *"Harataiken bahiren"* (The Harataiken Dancers):

> Tonight is the Festival of the Milky Way and the Forests.
> The drums beat ever stronger
> on the peneplain of heaven's end.

or in the poem "Taneyama and Taneyama gahara Part III":

> Mountain ridges rolling in countless layers, like waves on the sea,
> And the gentle, gentle swelling and falling line of heaven's end.

Heaven's end is the line where the earth's horizon and the sky touch, in other words, the horizon as seen from above, and such an expression could only come from first placing one's perspective in the heavens.

Kenji viewed his own position in existence as one point in the universe. As evidenced by the phrase from *An Introduction to Peasant Art*, "This is a meadow in Iwate, Japan, circling the sun in the space of the Galaxy," he saw his own position as being in the midst of the universe.

Surely his wealth and freedom of movement in perspective must have had some relation to his capacity for lightness. He must have leapt into space, crying "Hoho!" and, for one instant, soared in the heavens.

In the documentary film *Kenji's School—Taneyama gahara*, his student Yoshimori Neko recalls a song

"Taneyama gahara" written and composed by Kenji.

(Taneyama gahara)
Casts the ibis fire of a vivid dawn
  into a dream of Alpen farms.
Robing himself in straw cords and linden trees,
  he makes his vow to the wind and light.
When the sweet scented south wind blows over the grasses
  on the Milla-fire plateau
  where cloud shadows cross the meadow,
He burns the fire of dawn.

Looking down from the cosmos, the plateau of Taneyama gahara with its cloud shadows crossing the grass appears like fire on a variable star, or in Kenji's words, like a "Milla-fire plateau." He looks at it from the perspective of the stars, the heavens and the earth woven into one great festival of nature, and the prayers of the people who live there and tend the alpen farms.

It is not just his feelings that soar in the heavens. Sometimes the things that appear in his works also climb into space.

The train in his story *"Ginga tetsudo no yoru"* (The Galactic Railroad) and the nighthawk in "The Nighthawk Star" both aim toward the stars, and in "The Pasque-Flowers" the souls of two flowers aspire heavenward. These, too, must have some relation to Kenji's lightness.

Becoming Clouds, Grass, and Sunlight

Countless clouds appear in Kenji's works. They move and change as if they were living creatures. A famous poem by Bocho Yamamura addresses clouds in the following way:

Hey! Clouds!
Moving so leisurely,
You seem outrageously carefree.
Where are you going?
All the way to Iwakidaira?

Kenji's clouds, however, are not simply part of the scenery. For example, in "The Frog's Rubber Boots" there is a scene in which the three frogs, Kan, Bun, and, Ben, are cloud-gazing. Just as we might watch the moon or view cherry blossoms, they enjoy the clouds, conversing as follows:

"That really is a splendid cloud, isn't it? It's gradually becoming a petena."

"Yes. It's a light gold. It makes me think of eternal life."

"It's just perfect, isn't it?"

The ridge of the cloud moved closer gradually forming a petena shape.

Kenji goes on to explain that "petena" in frog language refers to a flat shape and that it is a very refined word. This captures some of his profound sense of humor, but of particular interest is the fact that the frogs' remarks of "It really is splendid, isn't it?", "It makes me think of eternal life," and "It's just perfect" as they watch the clouds floating in the sky, endlessly changing shape and color, voice Kenji's own thoughts concerning clouds.

Soon after Kenji was appointed to the Agricultural School he wrote the following "*Seishinka*" (Spirit Song) for his students as they did not yet have a school song.

> The sun reigns, and its shining
> Pours down a white-gold rain.
> We bend low to the black earth
> And sow the seeds of the plant of truth.

Beneath the brilliant streaming sunlight, we sow the seeds of the plant of truth in the fertile soil, sweating as we toil. The sun is the source of all life. In this extremely simple design of nature and human toil, clouds are not specifically mentioned. However, the sun makes clouds and causes the white-gold rain to fall upon the earth. In this tranquil, peaceful scene, clouds are clearly praised as a movement of the heavens.

In a previous section I referred to the conversation between two cloud-gazing pasque-flowers. Their conversation continues as follows:

> "It's coming. It's coming. Oh! It's dark! Everything has suddenly turned blue and silent."
> "Yes, but half the cloud has gone beneath the sun. It will soon become light again."

"The sun's coming out. Ah! It's bright again."

"It's no good. Another one's coming. Look, that poplar over there is turning black."

"Yes. It's like a kaleidoscope, isn't it?"

"Oh! Look! A cloud shadow is sliding down the snow on the mountaintop. Over there. See? It's moving slower than over here."

"It's coming down now. Ah! It's going fast, faster, like it's falling. It's already at the foot of the mountain. Hey, where did it go? I can't see it anymore."

"How strange. I wonder where the clouds come from. See, the western sky is blue and bright and very clear. And the wind is blowing across the sky. Yet even so the clouds never completely disappear."

"No, no, the clouds boil up from over there. See, a tiny, little piece of cloud just drifted out. It will grow bigger, you'll see."

"Ah! You're right. It's already growing. It's as big as a rabbit now."

"It's coming this way quickly. Fast, faster. It's bigger, as big as a polar bear."

"The sun is going to be covered again. It's going to get dark. It's so beautiful. Ah, how beautiful! The border of the cloud looks like it has been decorated with rainbows."

A cloud flows across the sky making shadows. Another cloud forms, floats across the sky and makes yet another shadow. Is there any other literature in which the beauty of clouds and their movement, like some living creature changing its shape as it flows, is so aptly expressed in a conversation?

The fact that the two pasque-flowers find the clouds' gradual changing and flowing to be mysterious and exciting, inspiring their spirits, indicates that this is how Kenji himself saw them. His student Neko's memory of lying on a bed of white clover with him and his exclamation, "Isn't this great, Neko?" as he gazed up at the white clouds drifting in a clear blue sky, was mentioned earlier. I am certain that at that time Kenji had become a cloud, that he experienced the clouds as himself and himself as the clouds.

And not only clouds. Kenji became the wind, and the flowers fluttering in the breeze. Let's take another look at "The Pasque-Flowers."

The two flowers have turned into tufts of down trembling as they prepare to take flight on the wind. A skylark happens by and addresses them.

"Hello. It's lovely weather, isn't it? And how are you? You must be ready to fly."

"Yes, we're going far away. We've been watching the wind to see which breeze will carry us there."

"And how do you feel about that? Are you loath to go?"

"Not at all. Our work is finished."

The conversation continues a little longer in this vein and then a wind comes to take them.

A beautiful translucent wind approached. First it fluttered the poplar opposite, then it made waves through a field of oats and began to climb the hill.

The two pasque-flowers shone and trembled as if they were dancing, crying out,

"Goodbye, Skylark! Goodbye, everyone! Thank you, sun!"

And then, like a star bursting, they scattered, and each single silver tuft of down shone pure white and flew off like a winged insect to the north. The skylark shot up like a bullet into the sky and sang a short, piercing song.

"Why," I wonder, "didn't the skylark fly northwards in the direction that the pasque-flower seeds flew, but rather straight up into the sky?"

It must have been because the souls of the two flowers had flown heavenward. And when he could no longer follow them any further the skylark sang his farewell.

This work is set in Koiwai Farm, and Kenji's ability to describe with such beauty and detail the drama of nature which unfolds through the rebirth of the pasque-flowers on the other side of death can only be due to his complete affinity with the flowers, the wind, the skylark, with nature itself. Not only do his intimate depictions of nature tell us how he approached and felt about nature when he went to Taneyama gahara or Koiwai Farm, they also superbly express his sensitivity and the nature of his being.

He even captures the sun as if it were a living creature. Let us look at "*Iihatobu nogakko no haru*" (Spring at Iwatov Agricultural School) as an example.

Beneath the light of the sun that pours down upon them, students collect fertilizer from a night-soil reservoir and take it to the barley field. The work is an animated description of a rural scene, but along with this vibrant depiction of labor, Kenji also paints a resounding picture of nature rejoicing at the first breath of spring, like a hymn of praise in the midst of a festival of life.

In this portrayal even the light of the sun "roars incessantly throughout the blue sky." Kenji calls the throbbing light of the spring sun which reverberates thunderously "the sun magic song," writing as follows:

It is a red blazing of lithium. The Koen Bodhisattva's sun magic song roars mightily in the sky and on the earth, accompanied by tiny waves of violet, orange and red sunlight.

Then, as if in sympathy, the life forces of the plants begin to move.

Sweet sap the color of moonlight begins to tremble and shimmer within the willow, the birch, and the stems of the withered grasses beneath the earth, while inside the shoots of the faster-growing eulalia and white clover, tiny golden particles of starch rise and fall.

Everything throbs with life and change. Fluctuations in the strength of the sun occur due to the movement of the clouds. Interspersed between the sentences he has inserted musical notations for a song with a refrain that describes the gradual changes in the sunlight's intensity over time, such as "a corona of seven hundred sixty thousand two hundred," "a corona of six hundred thirty thousand two hundred," "a corona of three hundred seventy thousand and nineteen," and "a corona of six hundred seventy four thousand."

Feeling Nature Within

"People feel from the outer world that which is within their own selves. They cannot feel that which is not within." When I heard my son say this, I knew that it was true. We can feel warmth within others because there is warmth within ourselves, and we can feel coolness within others because there is coolness within ourselves. If we feel comfortable, it is because we are comfortable within our own beings. Kenji's being had many open passages for sensing nature and self, the outer and the inner world, which is why he was capable of receiving and assimilating so much from the external.

If we look at his works, we can readily understand what he felt from nature, what he absorbed. Kenji himself has written,

All of the stories...were given to me by the rainbow or by the moonlight, in the forests, the fields, or along the railroad tracks....When I walk alone past the blue twilight of the oak wood, or stand shivering in the midst of a November wind on the mountain, I just cannot help but feel that these things are real. I simply cannot help but believe that this is what actually happened, and write it down just as it is.

For example, his story, "*Kashiwa bayashi no yoru*" (A Night in the Oak Wood) begins with a scene in which a farmer named Seisaku hears a strange voice shouting, "Saffron cap! Kan karakan no kan!" When Seisaku investigates, he finds that the person shouting is an artist wearing a red fez who suddenly grabs him by the collar from behind and for some reason seems to be in a fuming rage. Seisaku shouts back, "Red cap! Kan karakan no kan!" The artist is delighted and says, "Well! Good evening! Snippets of silhouettes have been scattered across the fields." To which Seisaku responds, "Good evening. It's a lovely night. The sky will soon be sprinkled with silver dust. Pardon me." The artist, ecstatic, invites Seisaku to accompany him, saying, "Let's go to the forest. I've been invited as a guest of the King of the Oak Wood. Come, I'll show you something interesting."

When they enter the woods, the oak trees try to frighten Seisaku, shouting on the wind, "Sera sera sera, Seisaku. Sera sera baa!" Seisaku silences them by shouting back, "Hera hera hera, Seisaku, hera hera babaa!" The oak trees harass Seisaku because he has cut down many of their fellows. When he is presented to the King, the latter berates him for this and they begin to argue. Just then the moon rises. The King ceases fighting, turns to the moon, and starts to sing.

When he finishes, the oaks commence a singing contest conducted by the artist. An owl joins them and the party goes into full swing, until a mist envelops them. Disconcerted, the oaks freeze rigid while the owl flees and the artist vanishes. Leaving the wood, Seisaku faintly hears the sound of the artist crying, "Red cap! Kan karakan no kan!" and there the story ends.

This is one of the things that Kenji swears he simply cannot help but believe actually happened when he passed alone by the oak wood in the blue twilight and stood shivering in the November wind on the mountain.

The banter between Seisaku and the artist or between Seisaku and the oak trees is both nonsensical and amusing. The ring of the words they exchange becomes music, showing us that conversation transcends the meaning of individual words. The song party held by the oaks and the owl takes up an overwhelming portion of the story, but there is no doubt that Kenji actually heard these songs as he "walked alone past the blue twilight of the oak wood." In those moments, Kenji surely became the King of the Oaks, Seisaku, the artist, the owl, and even the moon.

In their infancy, children remain undifferentiated from nature, making no distinction between the external world and the inner world of their own selves. They are capable of becoming a bird, a tree, or a cloud racing across the sky. We lose this ability when we reach adulthood, becoming firmly confined within the boundaries of so-called "common sense," those rules that dictate appropriate adult behavior and which were developed to maintain our society's production system.

Long ago, in more primitive times, people did not differentiate between themselves and the outer world when they reached adulthood, but remained one with nature. Even now, in areas considered "uncivilized," animism, which perceives natural phenomena as the work of spirits residing in all created things, remains, and life is carried on within a union of matter and spirit where man and nature are one.

I believe that although he happened to live in a materialistic society, Kenji was similar to people in primitive times. For him, nature, be it the mountain, the plateau, or the forest, was not a place to visit but rather was home.

He loved high places and was famed for his tree climbing. If a bird alighted in a tree he would shimmy up the trunk to talk with it. Such actions were spontaneous.

When we climb to a higher place, our perspective shifts. People appear small and far away, and we are filled with a sense that people are but one part of the wide expanse of nature. Nature's vastness teaches us the futility of our bondage to the inconsequential worries of daily life. Kenji's sense that we should "one and all become as shining cosmic dust, scattering to the ends of the sky" (*An Introduction to Peasant Art*) arose from his affinity for nature.

For Kenji, the mountains were a reminder that human beings are not absolute but merely one part of the whole; they were a space that allowed him to feel the limitless power of the universe before which human beings bow down in reverence.

Assimilating Nature, Becoming Nature

In the universe, all things are part of one interconnected whole. This is what Kenji's being instinctively felt. The nature of his being allowed him to assimilate natural phenomena, to communicate with creatures inhabiting the natural world, a clod of earth, the wind, or rays of light. Other people might consider him immature, strange or incredible. But Kenji was impelled to express these things, "regardless of what others may say."

Regardless of what others may say,
I am a young elaeagnus,
Its branches brimming with
Shining globules of water,
Chill droplets,
Translucent raindrops.

Regardless of what others might say, regardless of what they might tell him, he declares himself to be a young elaeagnus, most likely meaning that his thoughts have shifted, have been united with the tree. He is looking anew at nature and human society through its eyes, seeing a different, new world that we must ponder.

In the eyes of a tree, the human activities of cutting timber and pulling up weeds must undoubtedly be difficult to forgive. In that instant, the plant's life force is terminated. Do humans actually have the right to deprive plants of life when they have come into being through the will of the universe? Kenji agonizes over this point. Let us look at the following poem entitled "*Zasso*" (Weeds).

The hoe moves of its own accord,
Unable to be still.
What a splendid aster,
Its leaves

Purple-copper like a sugar beet,
All tapering.
In order that a different design
Of tin-colored burdock or lettuce
Might blossom here,
I chisel away at this dreamlike, elegant arabesque
with its sporadically vanishing edges.
All the sins of defiling the sacred
Fall upon me in this work.
And in reparation,
Let me create some romantic lawn.
Let me take these dish-shaped flowers of golden wire
And spread them over an entire field.
   The darkness of clouds
   The brightness of sand
An eagle alights upon a shoal somewhere.

Although it is but a weed, the aster is very much alive. Kenji finds it hard to snuff out the life of such a heroic plant, even though it must be done in order to cultivate the field. The aster is shaped like an arabesque pattern found in Islamic art, and he sees himself chiselling away at this beautiful pattern. His action is equivalent to all the sins of defiling the sacred, but in reparation for this injury at least he can create a lawn of asters that covers a whole field.

In a poem entitled "*Kyukei*" (A Break), he again expresses his feelings about plants.

   Red clover and
   buttercups.

I am Brown Bear. Resign yourselves.
  The distant clouds turn into
  Loaves of bread ready to be sold.
Oh-hoho! Udana,
Don't tease me.
How could you tickle someone's ribs
with your naked blade!

Taking a break from his farm work, Kenji wades into a field blooming with buttercups and clover to sit down and rest. Yet it seems so crass to seat himself upon the flowers. "Well, there's no help for it. I am Brown Bear. Resign yourselves," he thinks and gently lowers himself. It is a tranquil moment with the distant clouds transforming themselves into so many loaves of bread. The south wind blows, moving the blades of the plants which tickle Kenji's ribs. "Oh-hoho! Udana, don't tease me." "Udana" is the term for a small breathy noise made in the throat when speaking in Sanskrit. In other words, Kenji perceives the south wind as a breath within the great living creature, the universe, and so the wind is also a living thing.

This was Kenji. His being had the capacity to feel and experience such things.

Chapter 2

THE CONNECTION BETWEEN
STUDENT AND TEACHER

Confronting the Ugliness Within

Kenji's rapport extended to more than the external world. His inner self was also the subject of his "16mm projector" eyes. Refusing to deceive himself, he trained his gaze on the Ashura within and projected this aspect into the world of his written works. Let us take a look the story "*Tsuchigami to kitsune*" (The Earth God and the Fox).

A beautiful birch stood on a slight hillock at the edge of a meadow. She had two friends, an earth god and a fox. Of the two, she preferred the fox. The earth god was violent, had messy hair and bloodshot eyes, wore tattered garments that hung like seaweed, always went barefoot, and his nails were long and black. The fox, on the other hand, was refined and rarely did anything to anger others.

One summer evening, the fox came to visit the birch in a tailored suit, his light brown leather shoes squeaking, bearing a collection of poetry in one hand. He expounded upon such subjects as astronomy and the birch, impressed by his knowledge, listened with rapt attention.

The next morning the earth god paid her a visit. "When I think about it, there seems to be so much that I don't know," he remarked. When he went on to explain, the birch said, "How would it be if you asked Mr. Fox?"

As soon as he heard this, the earth god paled and flew into a rage. He was jealous. The birch tried to soothe him but his anger did not abate.

Returning to his shrine, his fury and jealousy only intensified. Unable to suppress his feelings, he vented his anger on a passing woodcutter in an attempt to divert himself, but to no avail. "Forget the birch, forget the fox," he told himself, but he could not and passed his days in torment.

The earth god was extremely upset. But even more so, he was lonely. Leaving his shrine one August night, his feet carried him of their own accord toward the birch. There he heard the fox expounding on art. The flame of jealousy flared up within him. But at the same time, he was torn, wondering how he, an earth god, could be jealous of a mere fox. No matter what he did, however, he could not shut out the merry sound of their conversation.

"Do you have many books on art?" the birch tree asked.

"Well, no, not so many really, but I have most of those written in Japanese, English, and German. I recently ordered an Italian one, but it hasn't arrived yet."

"What a fine study you must have!"

"No, no, not at all. It's actually a bit of a mess. It doubles as my laboratory, you see, so there's a microscope in one corner, a copy of the London Times lying over here, a marble bust of Caesar over there. It's really a muddle."

The earth god could no longer bear it. He was filled with a murderous urge to rip the fox to shreds. The conversation continued. The earth god covered his ears with both hands and fled. He was so filled with jealousy and rage that he tore his hair, rolled about in the grass, and wailed loudly.

When autumn came, however, his heart had calmed and

his meanness had disappeared. If the birch wished to talk with the fox, let her do so. If they were both happy talking, then that was good. The earth god went to tell the birch tree how his feelings had changed.

As the birch and the earth god were speaking companionably together, the fox came along. He immediately apologized for interrupting the birch when she had a guest and took his leave without even greeting the earth god. The latter gazed after him absently, but then he saw the fox's brown leather shoes glint in the grass and, suddenly returning to his senses, he raced after him, consumed with rage. The fox fled when he saw him coming, but the earth god descended upon him like a storm and killed him.

The earth god is crude, violent, short-tempered, and lacking in self-control. Just when you think that he has awakened to the goodness within himself and is behaving beautifully, the flame of jealousy flares up, filling him with murderous intent. Juxtaposed to this, we have the hypocritical fox. A dandy, a flatterer, polite, and always wanting to display his knowledge. Both of these are reflections of the Ashura that tormented Kenji himself. The spirits of both existed within him, making this tale an honest self-portrait.

True Wisdom

In another work, "*Kenju Koenrin*" (Kenju's Wood), one of the characters remarks that "You never can tell who is wise and who's a fool."

Kenju lived according to the rhythm of heaven, often strolling through the forest or between the fields, laughing, and when the beech leaves shimmered in the wind, he could not contain his joy but just had to laugh aloud. People considered him a bit soft in the head, and the children always made fun of him.

One day, his parents bought him 700 cedar seedlings, and he began to plant them in the field behind his house. People ridiculed him and even harassed him, saying the soil was unsuitable for cedar, but he planted each one carefully and cared for them assiduously.

The trees grew straight and sturdy, in orderly rows, and became a favorite place for children to play. Soon afterwards, however, Kenju died.

Almost twenty years later, a young man who had left the village to become a professor in America returned for the first time in fifteen years. By then, the village had become a town and everything had completely changed, without leaving a trace of the past. The professor was asked to give a speech at the elementary school and when he finished, he walked with the school principal toward Kenju's wood. It was the only thing in the town that remained the same.

"Oh! This is just like before. Even the trees are the same. And the children still play here. Ah! Maybe among them I will find myself or my old friends," he exclaims. Their conversation leads to Kenju, and the professor continues,

"Yes, yes, I remember. We always thought that Kenju was missing something upstairs. He was always laughing. He used to stand just about here every day and watch us play. I hear he planted every one of these trees."

And then he says,

> "Well, you never can tell who is wise and who's a fool. The workings of the ten powers are very strange. This place should always be a beautiful park for children. What about it? Why don't you name it Kenju's Wood and make sure it stays this way forever?"

People who are thought to be wise often behave without wisdom, while Kenju, who was considered mentally deficient, accomplishes a great work. You really cannot tell who is wise and who is a fool. The professor is not saying that those who appear foolish are in reality wise. He is simply pointing out that "the workings of the ten powers are very strange." The power of Buddha, the will of the universe is operating through the work accomplished by Kenju. This is what is significant. The power of Buddha, of the universe, operates in all of us. However, there are some who respond to the operation of that will and others who do not. "To live strongly and truly is to live in awareness of the galaxy within you and to respond to it," Kenji wrote, and because he relinquished all desire, he was able to respond to and live in accordance with the laws and power of the universe.

Near the end of this story, he writes,

> Who will ever know how many people learned what

true happiness is from the cedar trees in Kenju's Wood with their rich dark green, their tangy scent, their cool shade in summer, and the pale silvery grass beneath?

Kenji's meaning is painfully clear today, surrounded as we are by an appalling amount of pollution and environmental destruction caused by giving priority to material gain.

The Foolishness of Comparison with Others

A consistent theme in Kenji's work is the concept that we are not capable of judging who is right, who is wise, or who is superior. His famous work "Wildcat and the Acorns" is but one example.

In this tale, Ichiro Kaneta visits Wildcat in response to a strange invitation asking him to "Please come tomorrow because I have a troublesome case to judge."

The conversation between Ichiro and Wildcat's groom, whom he meets on the way, and Wildcat's behavior toward him is extremely entertaining.

While Wildcat and Ichiro are exchanging greetings, the acorns arrive with a crackling noise like salt roasting over the fire, and the troublesome trial begins. The case is to determine which acorn is the best.

The acorns with pointed heads insist that pointed heads are best while those with round heads insist that round heads are best; those who are large claim that bigger is better while those who are tall claim that taller is better, and as each acorn begins clamoring and shouting, pandemonium breaks out.

"What a racket! Just where do you think you are? Silence! Silence!" Wildcat shouts while his groom cracks a whip.

Ichiro advises Wildcat, who is having trouble making a decision, "If that's the case, perhaps it would help to say this. The stupidest, messiest, and most incompetent one is the best. I heard that in a sermon once."

Wildcat, enlightened, nods and with an air of authority, pronounces judgment.

"Very good. Silence! I will now announce the verdict. The one amongst you who is the least important, a fool, incompetent, a good-for-nothing, and a dunderhead is the best."

Upon hearing this pronouncement, the acorns huddle together, speechless.

That is a brief summary of the troublesome trial. Kenji was not saying that the type of acorn described by Wildcat is really the best. Nor was he trying to claim that those who are considered inferior idiots are in fact extremely wise. Rather he wanted to emphasize how ridiculous it is to try to decide in the first place who is the best in comparison with others. To Kenji, everything had an equal station in the universe.

The Sin of Living

The universe is an integrated whole. All creatures are interconnected at the root of their existence and together comprise the universe. Therefore all things must be equal. However, Kenji was troubled by this point because the very existence of life precludes the attainment of equality. In order to sustain their own lives, living creatures must prey upon the lives of others. Is it possible to have equal relationships within this context? This was the issue with which Kenji wrestled, a struggle well expressed in his work "The Nighthawk Star."

The nighthawk is an unsightly bird, so ugly that the other birds cannot abide the sight of him. The hawk, in particular, is incensed by the fact that the nighthawk shares part of his name and insists that he change it to Ichizo. He threatens to kill the nighthawk unless he wears a placard around his neck with the name Ichizo and announces to everyone that his name has changed.

"Why does everyone hate me so? It must be because my face looks like it's been smeared with *miso* and my mouth is split from ear to ear. After all, I have never done any harm. Why, once I even helped a baby white-eye that fell from its nest. Yet his mother snatched him away as if she thought I were a thief. And then she laughed at me. And now, I'm supposed to wear a sign around my neck saying Ichizo. This is just too much to bear."

In his anguish, the nighthawk flies up into the sky. Insects dart one after the other down his throat. A large beetle struggles in his mouth, but he gulps it down. Another flies in and begins to squirm, but again the nighthawk forces him down.

"Oh dear! Every night I kill beetles and other

insects.But this time, it is I who will be killed by the hawk, and there is but one of me. What a painful thing it is. Oh my, what misery! I'll stop eating insects and die of hunger. No, before that, the hawk will surely kill me. Well, then I will go far, far away to the farthest reaches of the sky."

Having made up his mind, the nighthawk begs the sun to take him, even if it means he should burn to death. But the sun refuses, saying that as he is not a day bird, he should wait until night falls and ask the stars.

When darkness comes, the nighthawk flies first toward Orion, then the Great Dog, the Great Bear, and finally the Eagle, calling in a loud voice, "Take me with you," but the stars are indifferent and pay him no heed.

The nighthawk's strength was spent and folding his wings, he plummeted toward the earth. The instant before his weakened legs touched the ground he shot up once again like a signal flare into the sky...

Farther and farther he flew, straight up into the sky.

The light of the forest fire dwindled until it glowed like the butt end of a burning cigarette. And still he climbed.

His breath froze white against his breast with the cold, and the air grew so thin that he had to beat his wings frantically.

Yet even so, the stars seemed not a fraction closer. His breath came in great gasps like a bellows. The cold and frost pierced him like a sword. His wings were completely numb. He raised his tear-filled eyes one last time to the sky, and that, yes, that was the end of the nighthawk. He no longer knew whether he was climbing or falling, whether right side up or upside down. But his heart was at peace and his great blood-stained beak, although twisted to one side, was smiling slightly.

After a time, he opened his eyes wide. And he found that his body was burning gently with a beautiful blue light like phosphorous fire.

Beside him was Cassiopeia's Chair and the bluish white light of the Milky Way glowed immediately behind him.

And the nighthawk star continued to burn. It burned forever and ever.

At first the nighthawk believes that he has done no harm. He even rescued a baby white-eye that fell from its nest. But when he flies into the sky, filled with anguish at the hawk's threat to kill him, many small insects fly into his mouth and he realizes the truth. "Every night I kill beetles and other insects. But this time, it is I who will be killed by the hawk, and there is but one of me. What a painful thing it is." Recognizing his own sin, that in order to live he must kill, he decides to immolate himself in the stars. His anguish at the realization of "what a painful thing it is" to kill and to be killed is Kenji's own anguish.

In order to live, we must deprive others of life; but if we do not eat, we cannot live.

I, too, have been through a time when I could not reconcile myself to this fact, to the point that I could no longer eat anything. But when I gave birth to a child, I was finally able to come to terms with this by recognizing that the life within others is the same as my own life, and that this life is passed on from one living thing to another. My conscience was finally eased by the revelation that the continuation of all life is based upon reciprocal relationships. I was able to perceive life within the context of our essential oneness.

The Oneness of Existence

A perusal of Kenji's works makes it clear that he was highly aware of the danger of comparison. The words "never compare" are an essential concept in understanding him. Comparison denies the existence of each thing as it is and it is the origin of many of the misfortunes that befall us in our lives. In the foreword to "Wildcat and the Acorns," Kenji writes as follows:

In this story, a child sets off into the mountain wind in response to a most peculiar invitation signed "Respectfully yours, Wildcat." It is a reverberation from the inmost being of students today who will most certainly be compared.

"A reverberation from the inmost being": what incredible words. The depth of Kenji's aversion to any comparison of children's divine souls is palpable. If we could raise our children without comparing them to anyone, if we could tell them, "You are fine just as you are," "You are a perfect living being," we would empower them to live to the full potential of their inner life force. Each would be encouraged to grasp the divine talents with which they have been entrusted.

"Wildcat and the Acorns" and "The Nighthawk" amply illustrate how much we lose sight of the essence of existence through comparison, but Kenji's style in "The Wild Grape and the Rainbow" drives this point home so forcefully that it is deeply affecting.

This short story follows the conversation between a rainbow and a wild grape who considers himself to be inferior to the rainbow.

In the center of an old castle ruin stands a hill, and on a vine on the hill hangs a wild grape, as ripe and succulent as a rainbow. A large rainbow graces the sky, and the grape gazes up at it longingly, thinking, "Today, for sure, I will speak to the illustrious rainbow even if it is just one word, to offer the humble thoughts of one small grape tree on top of a hill, thoughts stronger and sadder than the blue flames glowing in the night sky." In a trembling voice, he conveys his feelings to the rainbow, saying, "Please deign to accept my highest esteem. I would gladly die a hundred deaths if it would contribute to your unsurpassed beauty." To this the rainbow replies,

"But you, yourself are just as wonderful. You are indeed a rainbow that does not fade. You are myself in changeless form. Why, I am merely ephemeral. My life lasts but ten or fifteen minutes. Sometimes it only lasts three seconds. But the seven colors which shine within you never change."

"Oh, but they do. They change. The wind will soon

whip the sheen from my fruit. Hunched in the snow, I will turn white. And in the withered leaves I will rot."

The rainbow, smiling, says, "Yes, that is true. In reality, there is nothing that does not change." But she continues,

"This beautiful hill, this meadow that lies before us, with each second they erode or are whittled away. But when true power is revealed within them, then all things, whether enfeebled, withered, ephemeral or transient, are eternal. Even I, whether I shine for but three seconds or cover half of space and time, it is the same joy that I feel."

There is nothing in this world that does not change. But Kenji's perception of life is condensed within the statement that "all things are eternal," no matter how little time they have left, no matter how transient they may be. All life lasts but an instant, and at the same time is eternal.

"But you hang high in a sky of light. All the grasses, the flowers, the birds, everyone sings your praises."

"You, too, are the same. Everything that comes to me and makes me shine, also makes you sparkle and dazzle. All words of praise in my honor are for you also. Listen. Those who see with the eyes of truth will never attempt to compare a king at the height of his glory with a single lily in the field. Because they have seen that glory, the kind for which people scheme, is different from true power, from the power of limitless life. In that light then, even a single mote of dust rising from the suspicious cloud of human pride is on a par with the divine lily which was praised by the Son of God."

What conviction! All things exist equally and there is no need to compare something with anything else.

That which makes me shine makes you sparkle. If the rainbow is composed of seven colors, so too is the grape. Words that praise me are for you also. The grape, like the rainbow, is beautiful and vice versa.

He who sees the essence of existence, he who understands the spirit of heaven, will never compare a king at the height of his glory with a lily of the field because he perceives that what men consider glory is different from true power, from the power of eternal life. He will not compare by claiming that a king's glory is superior to a lily of the field or vice versa.

If we look at these things in the light of truth, even a single mote of dust that rises from the suspicious cloud of human arrogance is not inferior to the divine lily praised by the Son of God. To compare and rank things means that one has already lost the eyes of truth. Not even the dust of human pride is inferior to the lily. And of course, neither is the lily inferior to the dust. This absolute, almost frighteningly earnest assertion of the meaninglessness of comparison must firmly and irrevocably shake the assumptions of our present education system which is based upon comparison.

A shrill whistle blew at the railway station. All the shrikes flew up in unison and shrieking like some mixed-up musical score, they flew eastward.

The grape cried out, "Rainbow. I beg you, take me with you. Please don't go away."

The rainbow seemed to smile slightly, but it had already grown so faint that it was hard to tell.

Then it was gone.

The silver light in the sky intensified and the shrikes became so raucous that the skylark had no choice but to climb into the sky and sing slightly off key.

The story ends here. The sky with its increasing silver light, the shrikes and the skylark are not mere props. They are depicted as being joined together within a single existence, participating in the same world of which the grape and the rainbow are also a part.

Kenji's belief that we should never compare arose from his intuitive understanding that all created things in this world are connected together in one existence, and are endowed with the dignity of priceless life.

Confronting the Divine Talents in Students

Six months before he retired from Hanamaki Agricultural School, Kenji gave them the poem "Valediction."

The triole of your basso voices,
Surely you never realized
How they rang.
That joy full of simplicity and hope
Made me tremble like a leaf.

If you could fully realize and freely use
The quality of those sounds,
Their countless splendid permutations,
You would take up the arduous yet shining work of heaven.
Like some famous Spanish musicians whose
Entire families became skilled on string or
  hammer instruments,
You took up the bamboo pipes
And leather drums of our native land.
But of the 10,000 youth in town and village
Your age right now,
There are perhaps but five
Who have the aptitude and power you possess.
And of those, in five years' time
They will have lost them, every one,
Whittled down for the sake of
  making a living,
Or lost of their owner's accord.
No talent, no power, nothing whatsoever
Belongs to man.
Not even man belongs to man.
I have not yet told you, but
In April I will no longer be at school.
I will be walking a dark and stony path.
Should your present power be blunted,
And the clarity of sound and purity of pitch be lost
  beyond recovery,
Then I will never see you again.
Because
More than anything, I hate

The majority who do but little work
And then rest content.
Listen carefully.
When you find a gentle young girl to love,
And countless images of light and shadow appear before you
Turn it into music.
When everyone else lives in town
And spends the day in idle play,
Go alone and weed the stony fields,
And from that loneliness make music.
The countless insults, your poverty,
Sink your teeth into them and sing.
If you have no instrument,
Listen, for you are my disciples,
Play with all your might
The pipe organ of light
That fills the sky.

Kenji's students were all over fourteen with the basso voices that come with puberty. To Kenji, their talk, their voices ringing in song sounded like a bass triole. The simplicity, the joy filled with hope, the way their voices throbbed with youth and life moved Kenji's heart, making him "tremble like a leaf."

He saw in each of his students a blinding brightness. If they strove earnestly to develop their talents in the field in which they excelled, each would perform the "arduous yet brilliant work of heaven." How Kenji longed for this. Yet he knew that

...of the 10,000 youth in town and village

Your age right now,

There are perhaps but five

Who have the aptitude and power you possess.

And of those, in five years' time

They will have lost them, every one,

Whittled down for the sake of

making a living,

Or lost of their owner's accord.

What a tragic waste. A teacher myself, I know this sense of loss very well, but it can only be conveyed to those who have experienced it themselves. Children with their wealth of simplicity and power are forced to adapt in order to pass exams or to fit into a society made by adults, and their simplicity, their talents, their power, are blotted out and locked within. What could be a more bitter loss than this? I am sure that Kenji's sorrow at his inability to help his students find their God-given talents and become engaged in the work of heaven was a major reason for his decision to resign.

Helping Students Find Their Divine Talents

Kenji used a single Chinese character meaning "heaven," "divine," "nature," or "destiny," not only in "Valediction" but in numerous other instances. He combined it in words that had such meanings as "divine talents," "heaven's work," "celestial music," "the heavenly gods," and "the sea of heaven." Yukichi Fukusawa, a famous educator, used the same character to declare that "Heaven did not make one person above or below another." It seems to me that we used to live with much more awareness of heaven, god, and destiny. Many Japanese words contain this same Chinese character. The Japanese words for providence, vocation, zenith, divine will, the laws of nature, destiny, innate disposition, and talent all incorporate this character. There was a time when we were firmly aware of that which was beyond our human power, when with reverent hearts we believed in heaven and divine providence. But with the "progress" of science, our beings became completely estranged from heaven. The Japanese word for weather means "spirit of heaven," while that for punishment originated in the term "divine retribution." In reality our souls still recognize the existence of the divine which far exceeds the powers of man. Kenji deeply regretted the fact that his students must forsake their God-given talents in order to make a living. The talents, powers, and material things that men possess "do not belong to man." They are not meant for people alone. Kenji further emphasized this point by adding, "Not even man belongs to man" most likely because he felt that his students were too ignorant of the relationship between their own talents and heaven. He must have told them repeatedly, "Nothing in this world belongs to you alone, there is nothing that you can possess," explaining that "not even your talents, not even you belong to yourself."

The concept of "divine talent" is incomprehensible to those who seek to satisfy such worldly desires as wealth, status, and honor. Such people are capable neither of acknowledging nor of manifesting their God-given talents. Divine talent begins to operate only in those who undertake divine work. If one idles one's life away, one's divine talents will atrophy.

When everyone else lives in town
And spends the day in idle play,
Go alone and weed the stony fields,
And from that loneliness make music.
The countless insults, your poverty,
Sink your teeth into them and sing.
If you have no instrument,
Listen, for you are my disciples,
Play with all your might
The pipe organ of light
That fills the sky.

Kenji's student Toshio Nagasaka gave me a glimpse into the extent to which Kenji strove to help his students manifest their divine talents. He praised Nagasaka, who played the role of plant doctor in a play, as a "brilliant comedian." When he heard these words, Nagasaka knew that that is what he really wanted to be. But when he returned home, his father refused to listen to such "nonsense."

If Nagasaka's father had perceived his son's God-given talent, many people might have enjoyed his performances as a comedian in the 1930s. "Whittled down for the sake of making a living, Or lost of their owner's accord." How many of our God-given talents remain dormant at the end of our lives? Now, when "a myriad geniuses, each one unique, must arise together, then will earth become heaven" (*An Introduction to Peasant Art*).

And as long as the divine potential of each individual remains unmanifested, the transformation of this earth into heaven, or in other words, the appearance of a world that has attained true prosperity, is impossible.

Kenji's words when he states his expectations to his students are severe. "Because, More than anything, I hate, The majority who do but little work, And then rest content." One can never develop one's talents in this way.

This poem clearly conveys the sincerity with which Kenji confronted his students, exposing his total self and relating to them as fellow human beings in the quest for the happiness of the world.

School Should Be Fun

Kenji was sincerity itself when interacting with his students, but he was not stuffy. In fact, the majority of his students testify that in the classroom and in his individual dealings with them he was a great deal of fun. He had a rich and mischievous sense of humor, and he and his students sometimes played tricks on each other.

For example, Nagasaka, who by his own admission was a great prankster, put fleas in Kenji's bed. The next morning a very itchy Kenji eyed his students as they tried to suppress their mirth. He knew that his students were responsible, but he never demanded to know who did it. Rather, he took revenge by playing a prank on them. Nagasaka relates the following tale.

Mr. Miyazawa made us watermelon thieves. He never called it stealing but rather "pinching."

One summer's day when they had finished their studies and were swimming on English beach, Kenji suggested that they pinch the watermelons growing in a field on the opposite bank of the river.

But his method of pinching them was completely different to what I expected. I imagined that we would have to carry them from the other bank, swimming across, so it would be impossible to carry two at a time. I reasoned that if each person could only carry one watermelon, then if the five who could swim went, there would still be enough for everyone to have a slice. But Kenji's method was only for those who could swim. It was Kenji-style watermelon pinching. They each took a ten-centimeter-long bamboo stalk, cut it diagonally at the tip, and shoved it into the watermelon like a bamboo straw to suck the juice. It was a prank in which those who could swim had fun, and those like me, who couldn't, had no fun at all.

Later Nagasaka discovered that Kenji had actually visited the owner of the watermelon field on the previous day to pay for the watermelons. In other words, he had specifically arranged things so that only those who could swim would be able to enjoy the feast, and Nagasaka who could not swim, would feel chagrined, a fitting revenge for the flea incident.

Of course, Kenji was also very dedicated in the classroom. Another of his students, Yoshimori Neko, explains:

> School is a fun place to learn. If a teacher glowers like a fiend, you can't possibly remember anything. Timid children will stop going to school. When it came to Mr. Miyazawa's classes even kids who were always late arrived on time. That's how school should be.

He goes on to criticize teachers today.

> Some teachers today blame their students and throw chalk at them, but if a student in Mr. Miyazawa's class wasn't paying attention, he blamed himself because he felt that any fault in his student was due to some fault in himself. At those times, the teacher did not throw his piece of chalk, he bit it. Students confronted with this kind of teacher reflected on their own conduct.

Personally, I do not like to bite chalk or blame myself because that puts a burden on the student's spirit. But the degree of energy Kenji invested in his classes is touchingly clear.

It is wonderful that his students can assert that school is a fun place to learn, that lessons are not a hardship. The voices of his students, seventy years after his time, are reteaching us what is really important to children, what it is that children seek.

In order to save the countless children today who are ceaselessly compared to others, beaten down and wounded in both body and soul so that they no longer trust anyone, both parents and teachers must free them from comparison and blame. Kenji's students all insist, moreover, that children cannot experience the joy of learning if the teachers themselves are incapable of experiencing it.

Education for the Next Generation

Kenji hoped through his classes and his relationship with his students to raise up farmers who would recognize the need to rescue Iwate from its wretched condition. His heart's desire was to train those who would combat the rural conditions that forced people to commit infanticide or to sell their daughters when consecutive cold weather and failed harvests left them starving; people who would work to create a more humane society, to make a new era. In his poem *"Seitoshokun ni yoseru"* (To My Students), Kenji makes this appeal.

You who in this age are coerced and compelled
Will you submit like slaves?
Rather, make you a new age.
The universe is constantly changing because of us.
You must move one step forward from mere exploitation of the tide, the wind,
All the forces of nature,
And strive to shape the environment.

Oh, Copernicuses of the new age,
Free this galaxy from the
Oppressive law of gravity.

Oh, Darwins of the new age,
Ride on an oriental Challenger of contemplation
Even to the outer edge of the galaxy,
And show us a history of the planet,
More translucent, profound, and true,
A renewed, improved biology.

Take all farm labor,
Carried out like a natural urge,
And through cool, clear analysis,
Raise it, with its indigo shadows,
To the realm of dance.

Oh, new poets,
Tap the fresh, crystalline energy
From storm, from cloud, from light,
And intimate the form that earth and man should take.

Oh, Marxes of the new age,
Change this world which moves on blind impulse alone
Into a stupendously beautiful composition.

Kenji devoted himself to developing the Copernicuses, the Darwins, the Marxes, the poets who would create a new and righteous age, who would elevate farm labor to the realm of dance and create a stupendous and beautiful world. His students' recollections are evidence of this.

Everyone looked forward to Mr. Miyazawa's classes. Even those who were always late never came late to his. Some students would rush out the door without eating breakfast, grabbing a rice ball to eat on the way because they couldn't bear to miss anything. If there was a difficult question that the teacher could not answer, he asked us to wait until a specific period of a specific day of a specific week, and he would look it up at the high school library, or even go to Tohoku University in Sendai, and explain to us the most recent developments in that particular field. He never did things by half-measures.

Yoshimori Neko

The teacher said in class, "Don't listen to what I tell you with your heads. Listen with your whole being." He had the habit of saying, "Some of what I have to tell you is even more important than books, so don't open your texts or take notes. Listen with your being. You can read your textbook when you go home," or "Listen carefully so that you can be a farmer with insight."

Tetsuo Segawa

The teacher never brought his textbook to the classroom. He'd say, "The textbook only uses examples from Kanto or Kansai, and all the data is from those areas. In order to become farmers who understand Hanamaki, you must learn about here. And to do that, listen to me. The textbooks will not help you.

Mr. Miyazawa was like a psychiatrist, he understood his students so well, but I think it was because of the type of person he was that he had such insight, not because he tried to become like that. He had such ingenuity that whatever the subject, whether it was fertilizer, English, or math, he could assess his students' condition and present a humorous story that centered on the subject, using his skill to stimulate his students' aspirations and lead them in the direction he wanted. I don't think it was something that he consciously thought about. Maybe it was just his nature. I think that in essence that was the type of person he was. He was just a playful and mischievous person.

Toshio Nagasaka

That man really dedicated himself to each one of us becoming a farmer.

Eisaku Sato

The teacher used to say that "Farming is the greatestof all occupations. So long as you have entered this school, you should become a farmer.

He told us that farming was a noble profession which supplies everyone with food. It is a sacred, life-nurturing profession. With that spirit, he said we should eschew any desire for profit-making, etc., and let the tranquil sweat flow as we worked. He likened farmwork to the sun, or in terms of Buddhist teachings, to saintly deeds.

Tetsuo Segawa

These represent but a small selection from the anecdotes of sixteen of Kenji's students which they related in interviews, yet his enthusiasm for, his attitude toward raising up a new generation of farmers who would create a new age is clearly evident.

Japan at that time, however, was undergoing rapid industrialization and entering a period of transformation in which many destitute farmers and their children abandoned their impoverished villages to be absorbed as laborers in industry. In the midst of such change, schools came to be perceived as facilities that would provide the qualifications necessary to becoming a salaried worker. Kenji's students were no exception. No matter how much he stressed the nobility of farmwork, this concept did not penetrate the majority. Of the sixteen former students I interviewed, only two, Tetsuo Segawa and Eisaku Sato, actually became farmers.

When Segawa heard that Kenji was resigning, he decided that there was no point in attending school without him, and he resolved to quit and start farming. He devoted himself to his work, following Kenji's teachings, until the day he died.

The teacher told me, "Talk to the rice seedlings. That is the most important thing." He explained that rice plants are always talking about what they want, so I should listen to them. He meant that I should observe them very carefully.

Tetsuo Segawa

Unlike Segawa, Eisaku Sato became a farmer reluctantly

because, as the eldest son, he had no other choice. He was so envious of his classmates with their salaried jobs and briefcases that he avoided them as much as possible. This was surely the true feeling of the majority of people who became farmers. But in Sato's case, the joy of learning had been instilled in him at school, and he began studying the Sugiyama method of farming soon after meeting its originator, Densuke Sugiyama, which started him on a path of passionate involvement with agriculture.

The Paradox of Being a Teacher

Why did Kenji, who interacted so enthusiastically with his students, quit teaching? His younger brother, Seiroku, discusses this in his book *Ani no toranku* (My Brother's Trunk).

It greatly troubled him that he should be idly receiving a monthly salary while at the same time urging his students to return to the village and become good farmers. I think it was only natural in terms of his character that he should decide to make his deeds match his words by tilling the soil with other farmers.

As Seiroku points out, Kenji's being, by its very nature, simply could not tolerate this contradiction in which he lectured his students on the nobility of farming, encouraging them to become farmers, while he himself received a comfortable salary as a teacher. Surely this must have greatly troubled him. And as a result of that inner turmoil, he resolved to make farming his way of life. He became convinced that his calling was to become a farmer and change the existing reality of backbreaking farm labor, to raise daily existence to the level of art, and to seek happiness for all people.

In a letter to his friend Kanai Hosaka, dated June 25, 1925, he wrote:

Next spring I will quit teaching and work as a real farmer. In the midst of hardships, I will be anticipating round green vegetables and fluttering poplar leaves. I have changed a great deal since I was in Morioka. Then I was always thinking of clear, cool-flowing water like water sprites, whereas now I want to step into the slightly mirky, lukewarm water that teems with microorganisms among the rice seedlings, or that flows merrily past the grassy weir, and thrust my arms in to release the water valve.

Kenji resigned from the Agricultural School of his own accord on March 31, 1926. The next day, on April 1, he moved to another Miyazawa residence in Shimonekozakura and began life as a farmer, living alone and making his own meals.

The sun shines, the birds sing,
Scattered here and there, the oak woods
In the haze,
Sing, too. Creak, creak. From now on,
I will have dirt-stained hands.
(Spring, May 2, 1926)

On August 16, 1926, he established the Rasuchijin Association and commenced his activities in earnest, opening offices in Hanamaki and several neighboring villages to draw up fertilizer schedules and making a circuit of farm villages where he advised farmers on rice cultivation. These services, all of which were offered free of charge, consumed the majority of his time and energy.

Japan was already moving toward the invasion of China and what some Japanese refer to as the 15-Year War, and gatherings of any kind incited the suspicions of police inspectors. Despite the prevailing atmosphere, however, Kenji held meetings for the Rasuchijin Association, whose members included his former students and trainees from Iwate National College, in the evenings after work and gave lectures on such subjects as natural sciences and his theory of peasant art. He also formed a reading club, held "concerts" where they gathered to listen to records, and gave practical instruction in rice cultivation. To ascertain what kind of instruction, let us look at his poem "*Asoko no ta wa ne*" (That Field Over There, You See).

That field over there, you see,
That rice variety produces too much nitrogen,
So cut off the water entirely,
And don't weed a third time.

...The youth comes pelting down the levee,
And stands in the blue field, wiping the sweat from his face...

Have you no phosphate left?

You used it all?
Well, then, if this fine weather
Continues for the next five days
Take these leaves drooping from the stalk,
You see, these drooping leaves, here,
And pluck them off.

...The youth, wiping the sweat vigorously from his face,
Still has the same bright smile like an apple,
Though he has worked a full year
Since we last met at the winter lectures.
Now he is burnt by sun and sweat
And haggard from lack of sleep.

And then, listen carefully,
At the end of this month, when those rice stalks
Have grown as tall as your chest,
Use the top button of your shirt as a measure,
Crop the tips of the leaves.

...Not just sweat
He wipes tears away, too.

I took a good look at those fields
That you planned yourself.
Variety No. 132,
You planted it well.
The manure is spread evenly,
How strong they are growing.
And that fertilizer, you spread it yourself, didn't you?

I'm sure people gave you a hard time,
But you need not worry.
You are pretty much assured
A yield of 18 bushels per quarter-acre.
Do your best.
From now on, true scholarship
Will not be learning out of duty
From someone who plays tennis while teaching for the money,
But like you, it will be
Snatched during a blizzard or a brief respite from labor,
Through tears,
Etched upon your being
And will soon send forth strong shoots.
Who knows how far they will grow.
This is the beginning of a new type of scholarship.
Farewell, then.

...Translucent power,
Of cloud and wind,
Infuse this youth...

One of the students from the Rasuchijin Association winter course pours his energy into cultivating rice. And Kenji carefully and minutely instructs him.

The leaves of rice seedlings that are given too much water absorb nitrogen, growing at the expense of the grain, so Kenji gives him concrete instructions, telling him to cut off the supply of water, and warning him not to weed a third time but rather to let the surrounding weeds absorb the nitrogen instead of the rice seedlings. He also encourages him saying, "Do your best." And gives him hope by telling him that,

From now on, true scholarship,

Will not be learning out of duty,

From someone who plays tennis while teaching for the money. But like you, it will be

Snatched during a blizzard or a brief respite from labor,

Through tears,

Etched upon your being

And will soon send forth strong shoots.

Who knows how far they will grow.

This is the beginning of a new type of scholarship.

And he prays, "...Translucent power, Of cloud and wind, Infuse this youth..." All things in this universe, whether animate or inanimate, are joined together, interchanging and resounding. The cloud and the wind have will. And Kenji's prayer that their translucent power will infuse the youth is a prayer from the heart for the birth of a new type of farmer to usher in a new era.

Writing Poetry and Stories as a Profession

Kenji sought a new, a true path as a farmer, and attempted to create with other farmers a new form of art.

In December of 1926, the year he resigned from Hanamaki Agricultural School and established the Rasuchijin Association, Kenji sent his father the following letter dated December 12, 1926, justifying a sudden move to Tokyo and seeking his blessing.

I did not tell you before, but I have been practicing the organ by myself every day in Sakura because I need it for writing poetry. I came to Tokyo to find a teacher who will correct my bad habits. I went to the New Symphony Association to learn the organ. The teacher told me to play, and with great trepidation, I did so. In the end, I played sixteen pages. The teacher told me that all of it was good and praised me very highly. So now, composing poetry and writing are both within my grasp. Please understand that this is not idle amusement. Whether or not it ends in mere play will be determined by whether it is accompanied by a persistent and honest motive, the abandonment of all passion, and ceaseless effort. Please do not judge me as indolent, rather let me proceed in the direction I have chosen.

In these ten days I have actually seen results which equal those of an entire year back home. I have been studying Esperanto, typing, and the organ, have visited the library and seen language records, have been to the Kikuchi Theater twice and watched Kabuki from the gallery at Kabuki-za. I will definitely not waste that which I have gained here. From it I will create a new structure and work with everyone to build a bridge, however small, to the supreme Bodhi to repay everyone's kindness. I pray for your approval.

His father, however, could not approve. His reaction was, "If you are going to be a farmer, then do what befits a farmer. If it were with your own money, perhaps it might be understandable, but what do you mean by gallavanting off to Tokyo on your parents' money to study Esperanto, typing, and the organ?" His father could see no connection between Kenji cultivating his artistic talent and the Rasuchijin Association and demanded that he return home immediately, but Kenji refused. Claiming that it would be a waste to come back in the middle as he would lose all the tuition for his prepaid lessons, he managed to extend his stay, returning finally on December 29.

In a letter to his father, dated December 15, Kenji wrote as follows:

Every day I stay at the library until about two in the afternoon when I return to Kanda to attend typing school. From there I go to the Symphony Association to study music and then from five I study Esperanto with a professor of engineering at a radio production office called the Kyokko Company in the Maru Building, returning home at night to prepare for my studies the next day. Not a single hour is wasted. You may think that I am taking on unnecessary extra work by learning music, but it is the foundation of verse in literature, particularly in poetry and plays, so it is absolutely essential. Even without your scolding, I am almost ashamed of myself for needing to devote myself so wholeheartedly.

I must apologize for the great expense incurred this time. My budget is as you saw before, and in particular, there have been unexpected expenses here since I arrived...I ask that you kindly give Mr. Kobayashi 200 yen for me, even just for this year. But I am made physically aware day by day how painful, how terrible, or even more so, how immoral it is to have no livelihood or fixed income in this day and age, and I have no intention of continuing to be a burden on your household or of causing trouble for Seiroku or anyone else in the future. I am not, by any means, weak-willed. It is simply because my strong will is being used to the full in other aspects of my life that I have not yet been able to concentrate my powers on such affairs.

The statement that music "is the foundation of verse in literature, particularly in poetry and plays," is a crucial point in understanding Kenji. To his father, it may have seemed a frivolous pursuit, but the letter conveys Kenji's sense of urgency that if he does not devote himself now to music and Esperanto, etc., then the road that he seeks to follow will not open to him. The fact that he pours himself into the pursuit of peasant art rather than concentrating on maintaining a fixed income is the result of his urgent need, not of a weak will or a desire to excuse himself. As indicated by his plea to his father to "Let me pursue the direction I have chosen," Kenji did not proceed according to a systematic plan, but rather was impelled to follow the path directed by his being. He did not waste fruitless effort pursuing some plan, but rather always proceeded in the direction indicated by his being because he could not help but do otherwise. That was simply the way he had to live his life.

Becoming a teacher, for example, was not a course that he chose at the start as his life plan. He had no intention of doing so, but when he came in contact with his students, he was inspired to walk the path of a true teacher.

By coming in contact with his students, by coming to know them, he personally experienced the depth of poverty in which these people lived. Only one or two children from each graduating elementary class were able to continue their education at the agricultural school, so the students with whom he came into contact were somewhat better off than others, but they were by no means wealthy.

At a morning assembly, one of his students collapsed and vomited. The only food in his vomit was daikon radish. The other students seeing this laughed sheepishly, most likely laughing at themselves. There is no doubt that his students' poverty far exceeded Kenji's imagination. The shock was so great that when he returned home that day he was as white as a sheet. It was through this kind of experience that he became practically and intimately involved in the problems of poverty and privation in rural villages.

As mentioned before, he often took his students to Iwate Mountain, but he always gave money privately in advance to those students who did not have the financial means to go. He did this with great consideration, telling them to take the money and then submit it to him along with the other students when he collected the fares for the trip. Or he would ask such students to copy his manuscripts and pay them for the work. For Kenji, whose heart was grieved by the destitution he saw in the farm villages, such actions were only natural.

No matter what he did, however, he was made forcibly aware of the difference between his own position and that of the peasant youth, of the yawning gulf between the two. He dreaded having his actions viewed as something apart, or of having people look at him with eyes that said, "Well, after all, you have the money." This fear was not limited to the issue of money alone.

Around 1925 there was a teachers' strike at school. Kenji did not become openly involved, but instead asked Yoshimori Neko to resolve it. Neko explained those events to me as follows:

The teacher had been a scholarship student at Morioka Agricultural High School. For three years, he got a hundred percent in all subjects. Because he did not want the fact that he was a scholarship student to overawe others, he asked me to do it. "Neko," he said, "I know you must be very busy, but there is a strike at school, and I cannot resolve it. Could you help?" And I said, "If there is anything I can do, I'd be glad to." We consulted several times and the problem was solved.

Kenji hated to be viewed as special, and in particular, to be set apart because he was the eldest son of the Miyazawa Maki plutocracy. In a letter from later years to his friend Hikaru Hahaki, he lamented:

In this, my hometown, because I am related to the social Defendant, the so-called plutocracy, when I do something that stands out, the majority greet it with antipathy, and I detest this. I have had so many bad experiences.

What actually bothered Kenji was his own complex concerning the Miyazawa family fortune which was built upon plundering the peasants. And this sense of being an aggressor most likely provided a further impetus to his efforts for rescuing the farmers from their plight.

Other than salvation for the farmers, Buddhism had no meaning for him. I believe that that is how he felt. But what should he do? What could he do? He seems to have recognized a calling to promote a variety of activities such as the Rasuchijin Association and to produce a wealth of poems and stories, and he threw himself into this work wholeheartedly.

Chapter 3

KENJI'S SCHOOL—WHY NOW?

The Kenji Within Us

Few people in Japan have been discussed from as many angles as Kenji Miyazawa.

Of the various people who discuss him, however, I am troubled by those who presuppose perfection and completeness, evaluating him in accordance with such standards. In other words, those who seek in him perfection, and focus their theories on pointing out his shortcomings. If a theory happens to include an aspect that has not yet been addressed by anyone else, the commercial success and popularity of its author are assured. And it seems to me that many people are well aware of this when they expound on the subject of Kenji.

Is it really necessary to seek that degree of perfection from him? If there is something that we can learn, why not sincerely investigate it? It dismays me to see people intentionally looking for some fault to criticize, something with which they can disagree, in order to promote their debate that perhaps he had such and such an aspect, because it reveals their twisted, unhappy souls.

Instead, we should be concentrating on what can be gleaned from Kenji's sensitivity which allowed him to perceive the world as one interconnected whole, and from his inability to do anything other than live in obedience to his being and express himself honestly. This could, for example, help free our sensibilities from the bonds of common sense or social consciousness, expanding and polishing them, or help us to articulate what we have intuited with our beings and been unable to translate into words. It would be so much better to associate with Kenji in a freer manner.

There are few people around us who challenge our complacency as he does, or demand that we consider whether the erosion, renunciation, stagnation, or deadening of our sensitivity for the sake of a livelihood is really worth it. Let us return once more to Kenji, come into contact with his works, and let his words permeate our beings. In so doing, we will allow him to awaken our awareness of that uncompromisable essence within our own selves which has been buried out of sight, the existence of something too precious to lose. Even more so, let him entice us to that great ocean of lofty words, and through their influence on our receptivity which has become almost irretrievably mired in "common sense," let us recover our beings which are capable of feeling the universe. In that sense, everyone has the spirit of Kenji. And Kenji is within everyone.

Even before he was born, there were many Kenjis in this nation. So, too, such people exist today, are still being born, and no doubt will continue to be born in the future. He also exists within each individual; his characteristics are there. He captured in words and literature so many of the things that we all share deep within our hearts.

Living Without Concern for Others' Judgment

Kenji was an extremely busy man. He strove until the day he died to develop his self, to establish a way of life with which he could be satisfied. Viewed from the outside, this might be Kenji hurrying about in the rain on behalf of a farmer, or Kenji trying to help an impoverished student, but all of these actions had their origin in his way of life. And he was completely occupied in following his chosen path.

For this reason, he was incapable of concerning himself with others' evaluations of him, or with whether his literary works would be recognized by the masses and bring in a substantial income. For him, such considerations were irrelevant. I think the observation of his student Eisaku Nagasaka, that Kenji was that type of person by nature and not because he tried to become like that, is very apt. Kenji did not push himself to work hard or to suffer for his students or for the peasants. He simply could not help but do so.

Nor did he immerse himself in various activities or write so prolifically out of a desire to have others learn from him. He was merely disclosing and giving form to what lay in his inmost heart, what he felt and thought when he came into contact with reality. He had not the least desire to have his actions understood by people on a superficial level. He was satisfied at the core of his being, and thus had no need to attract such unnecessary attention.

This point, that he did not seek to be understood by others, I feel is extremely important. Even if we remain unaware of it at the time, anything truly essential that is born from our beings will always remain with us. Kenji had absolute trust and conviction in this unconscious part of his being.

Wanting others to understand what you are doing is different from appealing directly to someone's total being in order to convey a message, or from striving to present this message in a way the other person can understand. As a teacher, Kenji naturally invented many ways to present his subjects in a manner that was comprehensible to his students.

He paid careful attention to their current interests, using trial and error to devise his lessons regardless of the instructions in the school manual. Teachers from other schools who came to observe found Kenji using ion symbols in his classes. They came with the groundless expectation that because the school was an agricultural school, its academic level would be low, and they were astounded to discover students studying at such a high level. This was the way Kenji taught.

The reason he was able to teach such subjects was because he perceived what the students possessed within their innermost beings, the power bestowed upon them from the universe. By appealing to this inner power, he enabled his students to experience many strange worlds which never faded from their memories even after the passage of seventy years.

He taught them things they had never imagined possible, such as the fact that each one of the 60 trillion cells in their bodies carried a record of the 4.5 million years of the world's history, that the river right before their eyes was once a sea, and that there was an age in which elephants and ungulated artiodactyls such as sheep, pigs, and deer roamed the area.

He used diagrams and excavated fossils with his students to prove these claims, and experimented with lessons that looked at his students' own existence within the context of the earth's extensive history. Concerning this love of learning that he shared with them, one of his students, Eisaku Sato, said, "He was a teacher who taught us just as devotedly outside the classroom as in it."

Does Economic Independence Equal Maturity?

Kenji enjoyed the rapport he had with his students and they in turn delighted in his lessons and in their relationship with him. Such joy is difficult to express in words. But the ability to feel those things that are difficult to express in words is a crucial point in understanding him.

Take, for example, Kenji laughing uproariously as he was drenched with rain at Taneyama gahara. His bliss could not be substituted by anything else. If we are to nurture a spirit that can experience such ecstasy then we need to understand the importance of experiencing things with our entire being. People who are incapable of this will expect Kenji to measure up to the rules of common sense.

For example, many accuse him of immaturity, pointing out that he never achieved economic independence. These people, however, judge him by the arbitrary assumption that someone who has not attained economic independence is not mature. Instead, they should read with an open mind his writings which he was able to leave us precisely because he was financially dependent. They are unable, however, to forgive Kenji his financial dependence.

Driven by the obsessions instilled in them by their parents and society, they live in the belief that to be an adult and a good person means to be economically self-sufficient. Their grief over what they have thereby lost becomes envy which they direct against Kenji who, despite his economic dependency, dares to do what they only dream of doing. Yet somewhere within them lies a premonition that his actions might stimulate some precious part of themselves with which they have lost touch. They express the condition of their own vacillating spirits by demanding perfection from him.

Certainly, Kenji had a strong father upon whom he depended financially. That was Kenji, and that, I think, was why his works came into being.

The selection of a path that wears away the spirit for the sake of making a livelihood: this is the ordeal touted as a prerequisite for youth to come of age. But is it not in fact directly related to the present misery of our society as a whole? A strange society has emerged which mass-produces this type of "adult," basing the standard of maturity on one's ability to generate material income rather than on the development of spiritual wealth.

The majority of Japanese men never move toward joining forces with a woman as a partner in raising children and creating a home. Instead they resort to threats, claiming that they are the ones who provide the money to feed the family. Earning money is the only thing that carries any weight and no one questions how mature a person has become in spirit.

The 1970s was a period in which Japanese youth arose in droves to oppose this trend. "Must we tolerate submission to the flow of society?" they demanded. "Must we content ourselves merely with being placed upon the conveyor belt of life that moves from university to salaried employment within a company and marriage? We want to have our own voice. How can we achieve this?" Youth with fierce demands such as these threw themselves into the student movement.

In that sense, the 1970s witnessed the birth of many Kenjis in Japan. At the time, an enormous number of people emerged who pondered the question of what is essential to humankind. The majority of them, however, went on to become typical "adults" in order to make a living.

Even so, significantly more people are now posing the question of whether this is really what defines an adult. Many in fact refuse to follow mainstream society, pursuing instead natural or organic methods of farming, working as day laborers in order to be involved in environmental issues, and establishing a variety of citizens' movements.

A large number of these people do not set off for the company each day, briefcase in hand. Some of them, for example, spend half their time working as carpenters in order to make a living and the rest working in ceramic art, in search of something that cannot be replaced by a steady income.

Even if they are able to live this way, however, their children must live within society and, in the end, will be driven into a corner and refuse to go to school, becoming so exhausted that they do not know what to do. The confusion that is now producing masses of such children is society itself.

If we do not change the commonly accepted notion that the only worthy human beings, the only true adults, are those who do not financially depend upon their parents, we will be incapable of perceiving what is truly important in raising our children. In this, Kenji was a pioneer.

His actions were the result of truthful and earnest obedience to the needs of his being. For example, he generously assisted students in financial need or those who became too ill to attend school, and at the same time, purchased records whenever he wanted. Such behavior is incomprehensible to people who believe that it is better to exercise self-restraint, purchasing only one or two records and using the rest of one's income on living expenses. What Kenji did simply cannot be understood by those who restrain themselves from doing what they really want to do.

I think one of the greatest problems in Japanese child-rearing today is the misery that arises from the parents' denial of their own needs, from scrimping in their own lives to save for their children. The majority of such parents feel that if they do not say something their children will grow up lacking appreciation, and so they frequently remind them of the sacrifices they have made, demanding, "Whose money do you think feeds you?" In the end, however, these words only make their children suffer, becoming a form of manipulation.

Parents who would not think twice about paying for their children's cram school or piano lessons do not spend any money on their own growth. And they continue to use words to manipulate their children, to keep them within their sphere of control.

The pattern of most Japanese parents in the past was to buy clothes for their children but never for themselves, a pattern born of necessity and followed for generations. In the midst of poverty, this was unavoidable.

This was even true to some extent of Kenji's family. His younger sister once pointed out to Kenji, who spent all his money on records, that his mother's shawl was ragged and suggested that he buy her a new one. Once it was brought to his attention, he naturally did so and his mother was thrilled. This indicates that a similar trend existed within the Miyazawa family, but in general, I think that Kenji's attitude was defiant. He viewed his parents' money as dirty and therefore sought to expend it.

Begging Children to Attend University

I once heard of an experiment in which fleas were placed in an empty water tank with the lid closed. The fleas, no matter how they jumped, only hit the lid and fell back in. After being left like that for a while, they no longer jumped even when the lid was removed. I think that the findings of this experiment could apply to humans as well.

Until very recently, landowner-tenant relationships existed in Japan. It was not that long ago that the majority of Japanese were serfs who were forced to renounce most of life's possibilities. Living with the certain knowledge that they could never become landowners, they continued paying their annual land tax without even contemplating such dreams. This continued for an extended period of time.

After World War II, when land reformation destroyed the landowner-tenant relationship, a person's academic record became the vehicle to power. Former tenants must have rejoiced at this turn of events, for now, with education, their children could surpass even the landowner's children. However, the liberation and exhilaration of being able to make a livelihood if one but went to school soon turned into a source of anguish. A new period began where parents urged their children to go to university so that they were immersed for increasing lengths of time in the comparative education system. They lost their ability to just be, comparing themselves instead to those who were superior and becoming incapable of acknowledging their own selves.

In the past, a far greater number of students went to university of their own accord, some of them even against their parents' wishes. Now parents beg their children to go to university, and studying has come to be regarded as a child's sole occupation so that the trend of recognizing people as adults only if they make money regardless of their inner development has been strengthened and become firmly rooted. And I think that this trend lies behind the spiritual immaturity of today's society. If we but take a glimpse into the society of our children, it is evident that it epitomizes adult society. The first thing that children want is money, followed by computer games, and then someone to pick on.

Many things that Kenji put into words more than seventy years ago are helpful as a reference for considering how to mature spiritually, how to develop as flexible yet strong beings.

A Mirror Reflecting Today's Restrictiveness

The trend to weigh everything in terms of money has also transformed the school into a very restrictive place. Whenever an accident occurs, it leads to the question of reparation. In such an atmosphere a teacher can only relate to his students in terms of preventing accidents. If a student leans out the window to look outside, the teacher turns black with rage, practically leaping on the student in his haste to warn him. And the number of windows with railings increases.

Schools are now full of locks. The science room is locked because it would be disastrous if a student got into the chemicals and had an accident while the teacher was not there. The gymnasium is locked so that children cannot hurt themselves when there is no teacher to supervise. After school, the gates are all locked. Everything is conceived only in terms of how to prevent accidents.

How would Kenji's relationship with his students have fared in such an environment? As previously mentioned, the activities they enjoyed together had many hidden risks and dangers. If he were teaching today, he would have been fired immediately. There are some who criticize him for allowing his students to do such dangerous things, but he did them in full awareness of the danger. He risked his own life in his relationship with his students.

When they went to English beach on the Kitagami River, for example, one of his students almost drowned and there was a huge uproar. In his work "English Beach" Kenji wrote,

If one of my students began to drown, I could not possibly save them. If they did, my intention was to leap into the water and drown with them, to accompany them to the other side of death. That is how much fun those summer moments at English beach were for us. And I never thought that what we did was wrong.

Kenji had prepared himself to die in order to ensure that his students had time for joy.

Some things that are really fun contain an element of risk, the knowledge that you could die at any moment. If children are denied this, then their wildness, their Eros cannot develop. I think that Kenji understood this point very well, whereas someone who is unwilling to risk injury or even death for his students cannot possibly comprehend it.

Teachers today cannot take their students to the mountains or the rivers because the responsibility of the principal, their caretaker, will be questioned. Kenji is a valuable reference for us in learning just how restrictive our society has become. I am not saying that we should imitate Kenji or duplicate his methods. I think, however, that his actions and his works are an excellent key for understanding the type of caretaker's society we live in.

Scrutinizing the Reality Before You

Kenji did not limit himself to speaking in idealistic terms of the far-off world in his head. In fact, everything that occurred in daily life around him was the object of his fascinated scrutiny.

For example, he observed with wondering eyes the knowledge of weather that farmers had passed on for generations, the perceptions they had gained through experience, and he had a humble desire to learn from these things. Let us look at his poem, "*No no shifu*" (Master of the Field).

I come to visit you, O Master,
Between the long grasses and the fallen grain,
Crossing the white gleaming water
Amidst the thunder and the clouds,
And find you sitting erect upon the porch,
Listening to the stirring of sky and meadow.
Day by day, at sunrise and sunset,
You make small mountains of the weeds you pluck,
And in winter, too, wearing handwoven flax,
Seventy years having passed you by,
Your back is more bent than the pine,
Your fingers gnarled and crooked,
And the rain, the sun, all your trials
Are carved like a map upon your forehead,
Your eyes are deeper than a cave,
All facets of this field and the sky
Are replicated within you,
And all changes in direction
And their effect on your crops
Whisper in your throat
Like the words of the wind.
Your face
Is so bright today.

Two thousand times, I prepared manure
Hoping for a bountiful harvest,
And now, just when the ears
Are ready to ripen,
Four days of heavy rain
Followed by this thunderstorm
Have flattened the stalks of grain.
But tomorrow, or the day after,
Should the sun but shine, they will rise again,
And we will obtain the results for which we long.
Because if not, the village
Must face another dark winter this year.
In the midst of the sound of rain and thunder
I stand silent
For words are useless...

...O, Master, if this happened because of me,
With my superficial study by mouth and ear,
Thoughtless as a bird,
O Master, expend your power of sight,
And all the power of your hearing,
To look me square in the face
And listen to me breathe.
In my worn white clothes of flaxen cloth
And carrying a torn silk umbrella,
I am,
With the assistance of all the Buddhas,
Trying to protect with my life,
The Book of Juryō from the Lotus Sutra
That you chant each morn.

133

Needless to say, the Master is a farmer rich in working experience whom Kenji respects. Perhaps he is a composite image of the farmers who exist within Kenji's mind. He revered farmers whose wisdom was etched on their beings, and saw himself as a "frivolous bird" having studied only superficially at school. Despite the fact that he himself had no experience as a farmer, he prepared fertilizer two thousand times on the basis of a mere four years at an agricultural college, pouring his energy into raising production, praying for a bountiful yield so that farmers would no longer need to sell their daughters. However, "four days of heavy rain, followed by this thunderstorm have flattened the stalks of grain." In the face of this, he "stands silent." If the sun but shines on the morrow, the grain will rise and they will obtain their hoped-for results. But if not, then this year, yet again the village will face a dark winter. Kenji voices his fears, yet is given courage by the Master's bright, untroubled countenance.

What Are We Living For?

Kenji was, above all else, sincere. And the more sincere he was, the more he must have felt that sense of helplessness in which he could only "stand silent." This feeling seems to have remained with him until his death. Just before he died, he wrote the following poem.

Sickness has come again,
On my forehead, death stirs.

Someday, somewhere, I will be born again,
My karma the same.

But my earnest wish
Is that I be blessed with health,
So that I may repay the kindness of others
And bear the sufferings of all people.

And furthermore, that in the midst of suffering
And countless sorrows,
I will have a pure heart
And the capacity for joy.

And now, death, come for me,
And may the countless pleasures
That never came to me in this world,
Be given to those more beautiful than I
While their health remains.
What joy this would give me.

Kenji feels that he must face death soon. Someday he will
be born again. He hopes that those who remain in the world
will be able to obtain, while still healthy, the many
pleasures that he himself could not experience. This would
bring him the greatest joy.

He strove earnestly, with all his strength, to follow the path
to which his being turned, to lead the kind of life he wanted
to live, to be the kind of person he wanted to become. The
words "while their health remains" relate to his prayer to be
"sturdy of frame," "never stopped by rain or wind, by snow

or heat of summer" in his famous poem "*Amenimo makezu*" (Never Stopped by Rain).

Until the moment of his death, Kenji continued to ponder such questions as "Who am I?", "What does it mean to be human?" and "Why are we born?"

One of his students still remembers Kenji's answer to a question asked by another student.

"Teacher, why are people born into this world?"

"Why are we born? We are born to ponder that very question," Kenji promptly replied. This is true. And he continued to ask himself this question until he died.

I feel that there are two aspects to living. One is living through the power of nature like the grass, the trees, the animals, while the other is living to ponder what it means to be human, posing the question "Who am I?", and it is the combination of these two aspects that makes us human. Through the integration of the two, and their balance within our beings, a richness of spirit and a zest for life are born.

That is how Kenji lived, which is why he was able to live with such sincerity. He labored each day, preparing batches of fertilizer, tilling the fields, weeding and sowing crops, until he was drenched with sweat and exhausted.

Many people when discussing him take up the issue of money, claiming that he was oblivious to practical matters, but he suffered much more than these people imagine. Someone who lives on a regular salary cannot understand what it must have meant to quit his job as a schoolteacher and plunge along that "dark and stony path." How many intellectuals have the experience that would allow them to feel what radiates forth from Kenji's inner self?

Accepting the Darkness Within Your Own Heart

Kenji was certainly not perfect. Rather, as you can see from his works, he harbored numerous Ashura in his heart. He fixed his eyes upon them and considered them to be himself. This is of crucial importance for living.

In Buddhism, the world of living creatures is divided into six realms: hell, ghosts, animals, Ashura, humankind, and heaven. In other words, Ashura rank lower than humans.

The murky, damp, gnawing darkness within himself was, to Kenji, the Ashura. For example, the anguish of the nighthawk in "The Nighthawk Star," his torment over the fact that he cannot live without preying upon other living things, was Kenji's own torment which he regarded as one of the Ashura within himself.

That is probably what attracted him to vegetarianism, but he was also aware of the inherent contradiction. Although he refrained from eating meat, he ate vegetables which are, in fact, living things. I do not think that he was satisfied with the conclusion discussed by the characters who appear in his work "*Bejitarian taisai*" (The Vegetarian Festival) that it is permissible to eat other living things as long as we do not take the life of something too similar to ourselves.

If we do not take the lives of other living creatures, we ourselves will die. Accordingly, we consume others, incorporating their lives into ours and creating a circle of life. It becomes impossible to acknowledge our own life except within the context of this circle. This is true of all living things.

Vegetables breathe carbon dioxide exhaled by animals, so they cannot exist independently from the cycle of animal life. In other words, living creatures cannot exist except within a mutual interdependent relationship.

Kenji continued to agonize over this point, however, unable to completely accept this conclusion. He fixed his gaze upon this contradiction within himself and projected it into the world of literature, which in turn moves our hearts.

Nobody wants to acknowledge the darkness within himself. But Kenji confronted his jealous heart and a variety of other Ashura. And I think that he was able to create such a variety of stories and poems precisely because he was able to see himself as he was.

In the poem "Never Stopped by Rain," which he wrote while on the verge of death, he writes, "Without desire, and never angered." Because he knows the desires, the anger within himself, he prays to be free of them. To others his desires may have seemed insignificant, but to him, they seemed many.

Watching and listening attentively, he understands,
Without thought for his own interests.

Kenji found it painful to accept any concern for selfish interests or the refusal to watch, listen, or understand.

Never praised,
Everyone calls him "dunce,"
Yet he pays no heed,
I wish I could be like him.

This prayer arises from his struggle with that part of himself that does not want to be labeled a fool, that seeks the praise of others.

All of these are the Ashura that nest within his inner self. Which is why I feel that treating Kenji as a saint, or expecting perfection from him, only leads one farther away from understanding him.

A gentler creative force capable of comprehending others' pain and suffering blossoms in those who acknowledge the Ashura in their own selves. In his poem "*Warerazo yagate horobubeki*" (Soon We Shall Cease to Exist), he writes,

Soon we shall cease to exist.
Until the day we die,
Just until that day,
Let us sing like birds,
Won't we sing like birds?
Weak ones,
Proud ones,
Already wounded ones,
Come and gather one and all,
Let us sing as we expire.

Most likely Kenji's father frequently reprimanded him with such remarks as, "You have no pride," "Do you think you can live on that?", "You have no sense," "You're too soft." And part of Kenji probably already considered himself to be a bad person. But this is precisely why he was able to understand the pain and suffering of those who struggled with such hardships.

In the middle of his story "*Kamaneko no jimusho*" (The Kama Cat's Office), which features a cat who is always being bullied, he inserts his own opinion, saying, "Everyone, I sympathize with the cat."

In "The Earth God and the Fox" his comment concerning the quick-tempered, violent earth god and the elegant, erudite fox is, "If you compared these two very carefully, perhaps you might find that the earth god was honest whereas the fox was just a little dishonest."

Even in such stories, Kenji's feelings naturally gravitated toward those who were judged by society as having no pride, or as being slack, stupid, and good-for-nothing because he fixed his gaze upon the Ashura residing within his own self.

After all, the first book with which he challenged the world was *Spring and the Ashura*. Within the vortex of the brilliant life of spring, he riveted his eyes upon himself as an Ashura.

What if everyone were to confront the Ashura within himself as Kenji did? This will surely be crucial in the future. More than any animal, more than any plant, humankind has wounded the earth, claiming ownership of the planet. Such ownership is mere illusion but the arrogance of it is even greater than that of an Ashura. It may be said that our failure to look directly at the Ashura within has formed our society. Now is surely a good opportunity to fix our gaze upon them just as Kenji did.

In Kenji's school, we attach great importance to confronting the Ashura within.

Cornered Children

Here I must touch upon how the idea of Kenji's school came into being, why we need it now.

In my thirty years as a schoolteacher, I aimed for an educational approach that would help children acquire the strengths they needed in life no matter what kind of parents they had, and I tried many different things to achieve this end.

When I first began teaching, children still did a substantial amount of work in the home. They were not yet as influenced by consumer culture, nor as disturbed by television. Therefore my lessons concentrated on looking calmly at their life experiences, including labor, and their inner selves, and by having them express this in written form, helping them to consider how to face their reality, gradually engraving on their being a way of life.

From a good deal before that, there was a movement in public school education in Japan for making education relevant to everyday life. In an age when the poor masses made up an overwhelming proportion of the nation, this movement took a hard look at reality and strove to develop people who would effect a transformation. This was the objective of the movement, and you could say that my classes were a part of that trend.

Through it children became aware that no matter how hard they worked, the structure of society itself would prevent them from having an easier life. They could stop blaming their parents for not working hard enough and realize the poverty of the existing structure. And they could begin to see that within their poverty they had wealth, they had the bonds between parent and child and a rapport with nature. Nature often appeared in the conversations and written work of the children of that time.

In autumn, the leaves of the gingko tree in the schoolyard would swirl to the ground in a great blizzard. The children would catch them on the palms of their hands, start to dance and swirl, and roll about in them. Insects or birds caught their attention. They would turn their face up to the sky and the clouds, the moon, or the sun, and they frequently responded to the beauty of flowers, and so on.

In the last thirty years things have changed significantly. Corroded by the obsession of society, school, teachers, and parents that one who cannot adapt to school cannot survive, children have become estranged from nature. "Do you think you can make a living doing that?", "Do you think you can become competent enough to work, marry, and raise children?" This is the type of obsession that was directed with particular force toward male offspring.

In the past, even if he was poor, the son of a farmer had the knowledge that if he farmed he could eat and he was at least able to see himself within the context of a slowly moving time continuum, whereas now children must race to fill their heads with equations and vocabulary regardless of whether they are interested in them or not. The amount they memorize is evaluated on a grading curve and we have come to the point where this is regarded as the evaluation of the entire person. In this system, the first to fall by the wayside were children who had difficulty memorizing or thinking in the abstract. Only those who excelled at abstract thought remained. Those who failed to keep up were either forced to commute to cram schools, or, if they had the energy, to rebel against their parents or teachers and be treated as delinquents or "problem children" while those who did not have the energy turned against their own selves, withdrawing into the protection of "I'm no good anyway." The parents only heaped further blame on such children, exclaiming, "You're hopeless!" or "How can you be so ungrateful when it is we who feed and clothe you!" The stronger the trend toward judging on a grading curve, the more the number of such children increased.

Meanwhile, what were the schools doing? In order to raise their grade-curve average, they tried to instill the desire to excel into their students by intimidation, selection, and a battery of tests. The teachers, managed in a competitive environment and competing amongst themselves, were no longer able to show children what was really necessary in life. And children, dogged by grades and exhausted, were further driven into a corner by their parents.

Rebellion was followed by violence. Children destroyed school property, attacked their teachers or parents, or turned their violence against their own selves, committing suicide in order to express their frustration at having nowhere to turn and no vision of what to do.

The Creation of Kenji's School

Despite the fact that children are expressing their pain in myriad ways, the Ministry of Education, the schools, and even parents have forgotten the vital fact that schools are for children, and have further accelerated the trend toward grade-curve averages.

Parents pronounce speciously that children these days do not work so they must experience some hardship through cram schools. As a result, however, children lose touch with the true meaning of education and an increasing number of children who attend school learn absolutely nothing. Adults who have never experienced the joy of learning remain unaware that something is wrong.

For many years I harbored a major illusion concerning "parents." I assumed that parents' greatest wish was to raise their children to stand on their own two feet, that the parent was the child's ally. I believed that if parents really cared they would strive for the development of that child's soul, would value their child's inner struggles that are manifested during adolescence in their relationships, trying at the same time to teach them to respect many different people and nurturing a broad-minded outlook in their child.

This, however, was simply a delusion. Rather, the parents' real concern was that their child should enter a prestigious company, one that would inspire the envy of others.

Many parents who criticize the current education system and society in reality want their children to reach the pinnacle of the very same. I gradually came to understand that their criticism arises from a sense of futility or chagrin at their own child's lack of academic ability and his or her failure to reach the top.

About twenty years ago I began to doubt whether parents truly loved their children, and to nurture a resentment toward them because they could not understand something so simple. When I first encountered parents who publicly denounced academic evaluation standards while privately bullying their children, I wanted to wash my hands of them. Just watching them was more than I could bear. I closed my heart to them, not wanting to deal with those who, while their own suffering was minimal, had the arrogance to demand of their children, "So! You haven't studied again! Do you think you're going to make anything of yourself if you carry on like that? Have you no gratitude? Who do you think has been paying for your food all this time?"

But rejecting such parents does not solve anything. Children's problems are all simply manifestations of the problems of their teachers, parents, and other adults. In 1994, I quit my job as a schoolteacher. The focus of my interest was no longer children. I realized that we had come to the point where if the parents did not change, children could not change.

I began to confront parents face to face, retracing their history. These parents belonged to a generation that had already grown up within the post-war grade-curve average system. And what of them? Their own parents, freed from serfdom by post-war land reform, saw academic ability as a weapon by which they could finally gain ascendancy over the children of their former landlords, and using the suffering they had undergone up to that point as a springboard, they acquired scholarship. The succeeding generation was raised as a continuation of that concept, and now those children are themselves parents.

When I followed the thread of history, I was able to accept that there is no point in simply being angry. Two years after

I quit my job I rose out of the depths of despondency. If we do not create a space in which parents can see the exceptional talent within each child with their own eyes, in which they can feel it with their own hearts, most parents will never be convinced of the urgent need for such education. I felt that nothing would ever change without the creation of a place in which all children (and all adults, too) when approached by a teacher who focused on their growth, could prove to themselves that they can give full play to their own God-given talents, a place that concretely demonstrated this truth. And that feeling led to the idea of creating "Kenji's school."

Kenji's Schools in the Home

For more than twenty years I had felt the need for a new school. I even searched extensively for staff and land. Schools today are swamped by an excessive curriculum, and caught up with such unnecessary tasks as comparing and evaluating students. Confused by the pressures of the excessive curriculum content, it is impossible for children to discover or manifest their innate talents. Under these conditions, Japan will no longer be able to produce the likes of Kumakusu Minakata or Kenji Miyazawa, nor musicians or artists either. This is why I strove for more than twenty years to create a school that guarantees the provision of only those things that each child's being needs, adding nothing superfluous.

There were many people involved in various movements to make schools, and although I observed them, I felt that some elements were lacking. One was a curriculum designed from the perspective of a person's being, and another was an approach from the perspective of the parent-child relationship.

From the time of conception, parents play a major role in a child's heart. But the parents themselves remain unaware of how very great their influence is. How many times have children repeatedly appealed to their parents, sending a variety of messages to convey their sense of helplessness. Oblivious, the parents blamed the schools or society for their children's anxiety or anger which is expressed in the only way possible, through physical illness, rebellion, or withdrawal.

Children reflect the heart and being of their parents. Accordingly, if the parents do not resolve their unconscious inner problems and transform themselves, their children can neither change nor free themselves from their suffering and grief to manifest their latent talents. It is the children's parents who seal their talents and abilities within them. And of course the schools, the society, and their teachers, also.

Parents are incapable of realizing this because the history of their own beings prevents them. This is why for several years I have been holding workshops for parents and their children. Parents want social recognition that they are doing a good job as parents. And because of this excess baggage they try too hard to do the impossible. By retracing their history back to their own childhood and confronting the fact that they themselves are not satisfied with their lives, the parents experience a dramatic change and their children become much healthier. In the years I have been conducting such workshops, I have experienced this process many times. This is why I stress that Kenji's school must begin in the home.

All people originally are interconnected. The more deeply connected they are, the brighter they shine. But I sometimes wonder if there is any other society in the world today in which people are so incapable of connecting with each other as Japan. It is impossible to become a child, or an adult, or a parent in the true sense of the word in Japanese society, a society in which people carry deep wounds from their childhood, never realizing their innate capacities, a society in which the majority can find acceptance only by becoming economic warriors. National policy contributed to the development of such a society, but it was the home that supported it. Therefore, the resurrection of true connections within the family is the foundation for any change.

First the bond between husband and wife must be revived. If the parents merely blame each other, they will only intensify their children's profound mistrust of others.

The most important thing in human relationships is the mutual recognition that each person is a unique and priceless being, the establishment of a relationship in which differences are mutually respected and appreciated. Many couples do not realize this or even think about trying to establish such a relationship. Rather they regard the other person as personal property and try to possess him or her.

When a couple's relationship is based upon mutual support of each other's efforts to develop their talents and capacities, then the desire to form bonds with people and with nature is planted in their children's hearts. It is difficult, however, to find such couples today. Neither party seems willing to approach the other for heart-to-heart consultation; instead they snap out lines like "How many times do I have to tell you?" or "If you don't understand, then forget it." In fact, this type of mutual respect within a marriage probably never existed in the past. It is only now when we no longer need to worry about providing food for our families that we have the freedom to question our own inner maturity.

It is next to impossible for a school to take children from families where the parents do not respect each other and try to draw out the talents that have been bottled up inside due to the parents' physical and spiritual abuse. Therefore it is first imperative to make the home into Kenji's school.

To begin with, public schools were never created for children. People are too ignorant of the fact that schools were made to meet the needs of the nation. This is causing the confusion that is so detrimental to children's happiness today. How irresponsible it is to leave our children in the care of the school without even investigating what function it was created to fulfill.

When a couple fix their gaze upon the Ashura within their own selves, when they live truthfully, accepting the differences in each other and free themselves from the judgment of society, their children's beings likewise change. And consequently, the bonds within the family will be revived. This is what Kenji's school is all about.

Parents should be aware that whether they want it or not, the home is already a school that will affect their children's heart's and beings for the rest of their lives.

Parents must strengthen themselves to confront rather than flee from reality, to restore marital and family bonds through concrete action, and from this basis, to change the schools and society. If they renounce this responsibility, there will be no forward progress no matter how much they may wish for someone else to build an ideal school.

It is of vital importance that we take action by first recognizing our own responsibility before blaming the government or society. We must acknowledge that, perhaps because we have left everything up to others, to the school or the administration, we have created people who cannot learn what is most important in life, children and parents who are unable to form bonded relationships.

As briefly touched upon before, one reason schools have become so confining is because they are expected to pay substantial sums in compensation should an accident occur on their premises. Teachers are forced to supervise their charges even more strictly in order to prevent mishaps, and as a result the school has become increasingly restricted. The word "incident" has been indelibly imprinted in teachers' minds.

Take for example a student who complains of stomach pains. Previously, a teacher would have put his hand on the child's stomach and kept an eye on him or her for awhile. Now children are taken immediately to the nurse's room because in the event of an "incident" people will demand, "Why didn't you take them to the nurse's room?" "Why didn't you take them to the hospital?" So children are taken to the nurse's room even for a stomachache or the slightest of injuries. By doing so, the child's natural powers of recovery are weakened. Moreover, teachers cease responding to the heart of the child whose stomach pain may actually be triggered by a need for affection. That is how far the schools have strayed from the essentials of true education.

If an accident occurs, the parents will insist that the school take responsibility. And in response, the school becomes obsessed with self-protection. Teachers are constantly admonished to keep records because they are useful in the event of a court case. This increases the teachers' already heavy workload and of necessity pushes them farther and farther away from their original purpose of educating the students. And all of this is related to the issue of money.

Teachers and parents both try to pin the blame for things that are inconvenient for them onto others. As a result, they are unable to shift their gaze even slightly in the direction of real reform. Instead of reevaluating the administrative system of the Ministry of Education, the essentials of instruction, or the present examination system, they attack the teachers or the principals who represent the closest representatives of Ministry authority. Because of this confrontation, these representatives with whom they should be cooperating are distracted from the issue of fundamental reform.

This makes it very difficult for the school to return to the basic starting point, the fact that schools should be for children. Instead they are being exploited as agencies for the development of economic warriors to support Japanese society.

The teachers' union, which should be aiming for reform, has been fragmented. The union and the Ministry of Education have both strayed far from fundamental education which should focus on what is most important for the child. For these reasons, Kenji's schools are essential.

Kenji's Schools in the Community and the Classroom

Kenji's schools must first be established in the home. It is very difficult, however, to foster a child's ability to connect with others within a single family unit. Very few families attempt to give their children individual-oriented education, and as each child lives in the midst of other children, the ideals and efforts of the minority must inevitably be eroded by those of the majority.

Be it computer games or television programs, if a child does not have something in common with other children he cannot avoid being bullied. It may be possible for a parent to be different, but it is much harder for a child. When parents choose to do so, a child is very likely to express his suffering in reproachful rebellion, demanding "Why won't they buy me computer games? Why won't they let me watch TV?" The parents' intentions are not easily understood by their children.

It therefore becomes necessary to create a place for learning that allows children to have a real connection with their community, a community Kenji's school, in addition to restoring their ability for connection within their own home.

That is why attempts are being made in many regions to

establish Kenji's schools in private homes, local community centers, and other facilities as places for learning, places for restoring our connectedness with all things.

At the same time the majority of children still attend public and private schools. Teachers in these schools can transform their own classrooms or their schools into Kenji's schools. To do this, they must adopt the spirit of Kenji's belief that "the happiness of the individual cannot be attained without first realizing the happiness of the whole world" and revive their own ability to connect with all of creation.

As long as teachers themselves do not restore the inherent synthesis that exists between their inner nature and nature in the external world, they will be incapable of perceiving what the nature of a child's being truly seeks, or what each child really needs.

In fact, a movement has already begun among teachers to relentlessly search for children's needs instead of training them to conform to their parents' expectations, and to change existing schools into Kenji's schools. Although they may not use the words "Kenji's school," many teachers throughout Japan are already pioneering in this area.

It will therefore become increasingly important to strengthen the ties between the home, the community, and the school as a means of nurturing parents capable of supporting such teachers.

One Last Chance

The motivation for creating Kenji's school was not simply

to help such desperate, wounded children as those described above. It also arose from the belief that these very problems can provide a key to solving the issues that currently confront Japanese society and the world as a whole. Ours is an age of rampant materialism. How did we come to this?

The system of mass production and mass consumption that developed in Japan in modern times brought with it cutthroat price wars in the business world. In order to recoup their losses, businesses were forced to sell even more goods, further accelerating the cycle of mass production-mass consumption. For the same reasons, they sought to lower production costs and expand business by rationalizing and extending their facilities. Post-war scientific and technological developments added further impetus to this process. Productivity improved phenomonally, and as a result, production far exceeded actual demand. This is the background of our present state of surplus material goods, and the tale of how we created a society that can only be sustained by continued mass production and consumption.

Surplus domestic goods must be sold overseas which requires that companies become internationally competitive. To this end, they downsized and implemented complete rationalization thereby reducing costs and accelerating the mad rush to export. This was one cause of the unusually high yen rate that continued until recently. Fearing that this would reduce price competitiveness, businesses strove to rationalize still further. Caught within this vicious circle, employees were forced to work even harder, and the incidences of death from fatigue increased. The causes of declining job opportunities and the higher unemployment rate are rooted in the same phenomenon.

Complete rationalization reduces real wages which in turn has a damping effect on domestic consumption. And if that does not slow consumption down, the fact that products have become much harder to sell will. To maintain previous sales levels, consumers would have to repeatedly discard things that can still be used and buy new ones. This does not seem realistic in the midst of the present recession.

It could happen if a significant number of spiritually impoverished people appeared who could satisfy the emptiness in their hearts only by continual consumption of goods. But people are beginning to seek spiritual satisfaction. As they become spiritually complete, they will no longer desire material goods. Consumption will further decline. And the economy will cease to function. We are presently confronting just such a period in Japanese society.

Despite this, however, businesses continue to mass-produce, gambling on survival. Like a car going up a steep hill, the present social system cannot be maintained without a desperate spinning of wheels. In addition, the production of material goods has led to environmental destruction and the damage has been steadily progressing. For decades, people the world over have appealed for a halt, but the situation has not improved in the slightest, and destruction continues unabated.

Environmental devastation can only lead to the future annihilation of our own selves. We will rob our children and our unborn descendants of their future. We must stop this process now and arise to build a new, completely different society. We must turn our hands over the next few generations to creating a society never achieved in human history, a society that can realize "the happiness of the whole world." To train people for this task, a new type of education is necessary.

We must hurry. We have waited until the very last minute to build a new age. In the conclusion of *An Introduction to Peasant Art*, Kenji writes, "What is required of us is a crystalline will encompassing the galaxy, enormous power and fervor." We do indeed need such will, power, and fervor to create a new era. Do we still have sufficient energy left? We have come to the point where people's spirits may be so numbed by defeat that no energy can be wrung from them. This is, of a certainty, our last chance.

We are at the point where child and parent alike must consider for what purpose they selected their parents and chose to be born, why they exist here on this planet called earth in the midst of the cosmos, and particularly why now. Kenji's school is essential as a place to rear those who will give priority to the happiness of the whole world and translate this thought into action.

Kenji's school is not the first of its kind. In retrospect, there have been many such schools. Some were created even before Kenji's time, and the Rasuchijin Association, which he established himself, was certainly one. Just as, for me, everything that I did in my thirty years in the classroom was Kenji's school.

At present, many schools or organizations both in Japan and overseas, although they do not bear the name, are in effect Kenji's schools. We must forge stronger connections with these people and work together to make the realization of all our objectives more certain.

We are fortunate as Japanese to have Kenji because he has demonstrated that we already have within us the capacity for mutual understanding, for interconnection. The spirit of which Kenji speaks is particularly significant today, and it includes many elements that we must ponder. Just as Steiner schools or Frenee schools exist in other parts of the world, so Kenji's schools would seem appropriate in Japan.

Chapter 4

KENJI'S SCHOOLS AS NUMEROUS AS THE STARS

Kenji's Schools Are for Parents, Too

We are calling on people to first transform their own homes into Kenji's schools. Many parents may think that the last thing we need is more schools, but often they are not sufficiently aware of the fact that their own actions have a much greater impact on their children's minds and hearts than any educational institution. For children, the home is more a school than school itself, and their parents influence them much more than their teachers. It is only when children do something that troubles their parents that the latter become aware of this.

Mothers often bring their children to see me when they have reached their wits' end because of behavioral problems such as refusing to go to school, violence, poor grades, lethargy, seclusion, or physical symptoms such as overeating, anorexia, obesity, or asthma.

By sending out such drastic signals, the child finally manages to create an opportunity for parents to assess what they have done. Together we examine what children are trying to tell us through their asthma or other physical symptoms, or what they are trying to express through violence. In most cases, it comes back to some problem of the parents' or within the marital relationship.

Because the problem originates with them, the next step is to investigate the parents' own upbringing. We can learn many things by reconstructing the parents' homelife during their childhood in a workshop setting through dramatization or role plays where all the participants enact various roles. For example we might find that one parent was kind to the subject's siblings but tended to pick on the subject and was often irritable so that the subject was constantly trying to determine their parent's mood. They recall with their being childhood memories, which had been relegated to the outer limits of their mind. Subjects play the role of themseves as children, their parent, etc., and as they change roles they begin to realize that they are doing the same thing to their own child. When asked what they would have liked to confront their parents with when they were children, invariably the subjects break down and cry. As they talk through their tears, their anger begins to surface.

Once subjects have calmed down, the next step is to have them play their parent once again. Through this they begin to understand why that particular parent did not like them. For example, they may realize that they are too similar or that they touched a raw nerve in their parent. And they begin to identify the patterns that they have inherited and are repeating with their own children. They realize that while professing to love their children, they actually hate them. And they recognize in this the projection of their own parents.

There are many parents who believe that they had a very good childhood, yet if you delve into their past some of them actually suffered abuse. The belief in a good childhood protects them from conditions that they find hard to accept. But it is their true selves, rather than the fantasy they desperately want to believe, that comes out in their relationship with their own children.

By retracing the past in this way, individuals begin to realize that the difficulties in their marriage, etc. are often projections of their relationships with their parents or siblings. For women, sexual abuse, such as being raped, or emotional abuse by a sibling, a parent, or a relative who was supposed to be caring for them is extremely serious. The incidences are firmly sealed inside and never resolved. This may cause a person to reject her own self and make her incapable of tolerating, physically or emotionally, any intimacy with her spouse.

As for men, a husband may remain too close to his mother, unable to establish his independence. Because he goes to work each day and supports a wife and family, he may be unaware of his dependence on his mother. But if we retrace his past, his emotional attachment to his parent is exposed along with the truth that he sought employment with his company to please mother, and that everything he does is inspired by the desire to be recognized and accepted by her.

If we remain unaware of what motivates our actions at the deepest level, then we will not see the problems in our behavior. For example, people may be uncomfortable unless they are in a position where they receive constant praise. They are unhappy unless they are at the center of everything in an organization. They do not understand what is motivating them to create a pyramid rather than a circular structure, and to strive to reach the pinnacle. They create confusion in the relationships around them and cannot nurture relationships in which each party can truly grow. Our workshops help them to identify the cause.

Parents' Problems Affect Their Children's Health

Every person, as he or she grows up, falls in love. Falling in love is an emotional state in which one feels completely accepted by, and tries to completely accept, another person. In this state, a person transmits and receives an incredible amount of energy, which is why people in love seem to radiate. At the same time, however, caught up in the vortex of this intense mutual rapport, they are blind, unable to objectively analyze what is happening within the other person. It is necessary to realize that falling in love is actually a kind of emotional ailment, one in which a person tries to suddenly and completely fill an inner emptiness that was created by unfulfilled dreams and lack of permission to be a child during one's childhood. Often the loved one's energy brings forth one's own energy or vice versa. All illnesses, whether physical or spiritual, arise from the need to restore one's being to normal functioning, and falling in love is no exception.

If people do not realize what they are seeking through this strong attachment, it will be difficult for them to mature into adulthood, and dangerous to become parents. When a couple reaches a period of stillness after the initial fierce concentration and release of energy, they must consider what they want to create together and whether they have the commitment to build a relationship between two individual human beings.

In the majority of cases, however, the couple passes from falling in love directly into marriage as though wedlock is the ultimate goal, without any awareness or effort. And as the characteristics in their partner which at first appeared to be dimples are more clearly seen to be pockmarks, disappointment begins to rule. When they live together every day, when they can have sex anytime they want, the feeling that they could not bear to be parted, the joy that overflowed from within each time they met, is quenched and they lose their affection and esteem for the other, and begin to doubt the bond between them.

At this point, many men take those feelings of love that had made them glow and direct them toward another woman or submerge them in their work, while women are often left at home on their own. If a child is born in this situation, despite the fact that it was first seen as the child of one they love, it becomes a burden, useful only as a means of keeping the spouse bound to the relationship or of filling up the loneliness left by the other's absence.

In reality, the important part of a relationship should begin when the first glow of infatuation starts to fade. Now they can stop to consider how they can allow each other to grow and build a new relationship, and whether they are both prepared to do so.

This is very difficult, however, because their parents did not model such behavior. Even if her husband yelled at her, the mother, in consideration of social norms, put up with the marriage while complaining and belittling her husband behind his back. This is the type of role model most couples have.

Though a couple may fall madly in love, have children, and make a home, their real concern is social acceptance.

They can neither control nor confront their own desires. When such immature men and women raise a child, it is only to be expected that they will cause their child suffering.

They worry about what others will think and maintain their home trying desperately not to let the cracks show. Children who are sensitive to parents' problems will challenge them by refusing to go to school, or with anorexia, bulemia, asthma, lethargy, or violent behavior. Or they may play the good child and support their parents. When they grow up to rear their own child, although the form may change, they will follow in their parents' footsteps, and if they cannot fill the void, they will never satisfy their soul's hunger or ease the loneliness in their heart. This is the kind of thing that surfaces in our workshops.

Children yearn for their families to help them. However, if their parents wield absolute authority, or if they remain out of touch with their own hearts despite an outwardly gentle appearance, children will give up because no matter how they approach their parents, they are never heard or understood. In our workshops, these children can no longer hide from the reality of their despair. The true nature of their family emerges from beneath the whitewash, and the child discovers the source of his undefined sense of loneliness. When the parents' problems become clear, so do the child's and the latter is filled once more with vitality. The parents are surprised to realize that it was they who had a problem, and are astonished at the degree to which they dominated their child.

Children Long to Manifest Their Talents

The more such work progresses, the more evident it becomes, even to others, that children perfectly mirror what is in their parents' hearts. When the child plays the role of the parent, he skillfully mimics his parent's every gesture and shade of voice. Like a movie camera, he captures and projects an exact three-dimensional image, including that which is invisible to a real camera, the innermost heart of which even the parent is unaware.

When children who have been victimized by their parents take on the abusive role, they are filled with a violent energy, throwing cushions and becoming so animated that they seem different people.

Feelings such as "I don't want to become that kind of parent" or "I never want to behave like that" strongly inhibit children, and such inhibitions must be lifted with care because they are also suppressing surrounding emotions. By repeatedly acting out those aspects of their parents that they despise, children are forced to confront the inner Ashura which they have rejected, that part of themselves that they do not want to acknowledge, and by accepting it, other emotions that have been strangled come back to life and the children's health is restored. It is unrealistic to raise children to be "nice."

Having retraced the lives of many individuals through these workshops to pinpoint those areas where they were not given permission to be themselves, it makes me wonder whether there are any healthy families in Japan. If the parents of a preceding generation have confronted the

Ashura within, overcoming each one to grow spiritually until they are able to live according to the rhythm of heaven, then their children will also attain a point of growth where they live in accordance with that same rhythm as opposed to that of the surrounding society. But in our country, the "average" parent adjusts himself to society, concerned with being socially accepted. People who produce creative and interesting work in this day usually had parents who in the previous generation did not allow themselves to be influenced by society, but followed their own path in life. Such parents enable their children to manifest their latent talents and to become unique beings with the capacity to perform the work of heaven.

In *An Introduction to Peasant Art*, Kenji writes,

Professional artists will one day cease to exist.

Let all develop an artist's sensitivity.

Let each find his own irresistible forms of expression in the field where his individuality excels.

At that moment, each one is an artist.

The act of creation is spontaneously intensified when the creative impulse flows irrepressibly from the Self.

During this period, others will surely provide for his daily needs.

When the creative flow ceases, the artist will return to the land

Where many a liberated genius may be found.

A myriad geniuses, each one unique, must stand together.

Then will earth become heaven.

The objective of Kenji's school is to assist children, those "myriad geniuses, each one unique," to manifest their divine talents.

In what field does their "individuality excel"? What is the history and present reality of children today who cannot "develop an artist's sensitivity," despite the fact that "each one is an artist"? We focus on these aspects and on the fact that the child himself cannot even imagine his own capacity. If he is to tap his potential, the child must first become aware of it, and those around him must have the ability to discover it, too.

When we look at the children of the world from the perspective of their innate talents, we will come to understand that all children live with the longing to manifest their potential. We will come to see that this is the objective human beings yearn to achieve in their lives. It becomes possible, for example, to perceive a child's refusal to go to school as an expression of his longing to follow where his talents lead him. In other words, he has already perceived that school cannot help him to develop his true self. And he knows that he does not want to live his life in response to the judgment of the society around him.

Being Faithful to One's Divine Potential

Recently I met a pianist whom I consider to be a genius. He rejected the school system, quitting during junior high. Subsequently, he experienced many different things, but throughout it all he remained convinced that he was a failure.

I asked him to accompany my narration of Kenji's

"Valediction" and *Inasaku sowa* (The Rice Episode) by playing his impressions on the piano. He was no ordinary pianist.

Incapable of adjusting to what we call "school," he had quit and set off to roam the world. On this journey, he tasted our planet's inexpressible despair, a despair that he transposed into sound and connected with his work. His travels were essentially his education, the world his school. I am convinced that his rebellion against his parents, who incidentally were very rich, and his rejection of school represented his attempts to manifest his innate talents.

Any sickness or delinquent behavior exhibited by children can be viewed as a painful expression of their desire to fulfill their potential instead of being swept along by society. As adults, we must realize how important it is for children to become aware, just as Kenji did when he graduated from middle school, of their divine talents and to move toward their development.

In Japan today, many people search for the meaning of life in numerous religious sects. This is fine in itself, but we must realize that dependence on someone else in the quest for one's path in life is accompanied by the inherent risk of being led drastically astray.

The pianist mentioned previously did not cling to anyone else, but rather aimed to make music with which he himself could be satisfied. Consequently, he is poor, receiving only a pittance for his work. But he is being faithful to his God-given talents. People who manifest their divine potential cannot help but do so.

Those whom we call geniuses, be they Mozart or some

other, are generally recognized as such only after they have died. To be a genius means to live in accordance with the rhythm of heaven, and therefore they will remain misunderstood until the majority of people approach this rhythm.

What Kenji's school aims for is the emergence of "many liberated geniuses," "a myriad geniuses, each one unique" with "an artist's sensitivity." As they develop their own capacities, they will be able to mutually appreciate each other's individuality. We are aiming for the advent of such an age and feel that the world as a whole is now moving in that very direction.

A Mother Encounters the Wounded Child Within

I received a letter from a mother who confessed that she was exhausted from pushing her child to do his homework every day. The scenario went something like this.

As soon as the child enters the door after returning from school, she demands, "Do you have any homework today?"

"No," her son replies.

"That's impossible," she scolds. "Let me see your notebook. There you see. I thought so. You have homework, now get to it."

That is the way it always begins and from there things just get worse.

"Can't you even do this? You just studied it yesterday. You never listen to the teacher."

"But I don't get it."

"What do you mean you don't get it? You did it yesterday."

Her child wants to go out to play. But if a friend phones the mother says, "He's studying right now. Maybe another time." At this her son begins to cry. When he asks, "How come you let my younger brother play, and always pick on me?" she jumps on him, retorting, "You have to study twice as hard as other people." He starts to tire and she begins to get frustrated. When he makes a mistake she erases it so vigorously that she rips the paper, which only makes her angrier.

When her mother-in-law interrupts to say, "What about supper?" she turns on her child.

"Now look," she complains. "Thanks to you she gets mad at me. Because of you I'm late making dinner."

Everyone becomes increasingly irritated until even the father-in-law intervenes. "Just give up, will you? Even with your help, he won't be able to do it anyway."

"What are you talking about? Child-rearing is much more difficult than it was in your day, so don't interfere," the mother responds and then snaps at her child, "Look what your grandfather said. It's all your fault."

In her letter, she wrote, "This goes on until eleven thirty at night. It continues even after my husband gets home. I don't understand why I do this. Please help me."

I decided to work with her. When I asked her to tell me about the most painful memory in her life, she described an incident in third grade when she, who always got As or Bs, brought home a C on her report card and was severely rebuked by her mother. We then reenacted the incident with the other workshop members. First we set up the classroom and had one member play the teacher while the remainder became her classmates and she became herself as a third grader.

The teacher announced that summer holidays would commence tomorrow, gave them various instructions, and then said, "Now, here are your report cards." The woman, who had completely reverted to her third-grade self, was sitting nervously on her chair. When she received her report card and sneaked a peek, the inexpressible horror that she had felt at the time was revealed. Glancing around, she surreptitiously slipped the report card into her bag, then began walking home staring at the ground. But she was too afraid to go straight there.

She walked around her house, then sat on the riverbank until dark. You could see the reluctance on her face. She managed at last to reach home, but this time she could not open the door. After hesitating for some time, she finally made up her mind and went in, shouting, "I'm sorry."

"I'll study, Mom, I promise," she blurted out to the towering figure who played her mother. "I'm so sorry. Please, please forgive me. I'll go study right now."

"Then do so. Because any child who would get such a low mark is not fit to be called human."

With these horrible words flung after her, she began studying. This pattern continued until university.

Next she played the role of her mother, and another person played the role of herself as a child. This time, vicious statements flooded from her lips in her mother's tone of voice. In response, the person playing her child pleaded, "Mother, you never make my brother do any studying. Why do you always pick on me?" These were the very words that the woman's own child had addressed to her. I asked her, "Did you notice something?"

"Oh! I'm doing the same thing that my mother did to me." She had realized it for the first time.

We continued working together, and this time she played her mother as a child.

Although her mother had excelled academically, she was not allowed to continue her studies at university. On the other hand, one of her friends who received lower marks not only went on to university, but later was employed by a company and paid a decent wage. The resentment she felt at not being allowed to continue her studies rankled when she saw this, and she raised her children determined to allow them to go to university at any cost. The woman discovered, however, that in fact her mother's frustration and resentment against her parents had actually been turned on her.

"I never, ever experienced the joy of learning," she said. She graduated from university but married immediately. This was an unconscious act of revenge against her mother. Her anguish became even more apparent to me when I learned that she had once told her mother, "You forced me to study all the time, but now that I'm married I don't exactly walk around with the university's name written on my back or anything. All that studying was just a waste of time."

But her resentment remained unresolved. And so, although rationally she thought that she did not want to push her child because she herself had suffered so much by being forced to study, the unresolved resentment that filled her being was directed unconsciously against her son. When she recognized the structure of this relationship within her, she finally realized what she was doing to her child.

That night she returned home and told her husband what she had learned in the workshop and found that he understood her suffering very well. The next day she came to me and said, "I feel like I weigh half as much as yesterday. I feel so light."

That was the degree of her suffering. She had been carrying a very heavy load.

I introduced her case in a booklet entitled *Datsu "Iioya"* (Formerly a "Good Parent") where I referred to her as "C." After reading it she sent me the following letter.

"I read your booklet. I am C who forces her child to study. How short each day seemed before."

Up until the workshop, she had started off the morning worrying about what her child's homework would be that day. When it was time for the child to arrive home, she would become agitated, wondering why he wasn't home yet. Then, when he did come home, she would nag him to do his homework, glaring constantly at the clock, and groaning inwardly because it was already six, then seven, then eight. She neglected her younger son, rushing frantically to prepare supper and baths and put her children to bed so that each day was over before she knew it. Concerning her present life, she wrote, "How long are the hours I have for myself."

When her child comes home from school, he begins studying on his own. He is able to solve most problems himself and asks his mother only when necessary.

"It is so easy that I wonder if this is really all right. And my child's words are so fresh. I am sure he always talked to me like this but I was unable to even hear him." Her happiness is readily apparent.

When her child caught a cold and went to the doctor, he said, "I hope we can get some medicine and leave soon. I want to be at school for the science class in third period."

"I doubted my ears for an instant," his mother writes. "I am ashamed of myself for the way I used to assume he hated school and only liked school excursions."

That was how little she knew her own child.

Now his friends come to their house to play. He makes plans with them at school or calls them up when he gets home, and he seems very content. He confides in his mother about many things, concerning school, his friends, his teachers. "It's a wonderful thing to be able to trust your child," she writes. She is experiencing how greatly a child can change when one's way of responding to him changes.

In the summer holidays, her child decided to try swimming 100 meters. She must have thought him a little strange for setting such a goal when he could not even swim yet. But again she writes, "Despite that, he did it. I was drenched with water and tears."

If parents change, their children will continue to change. And they will challenge their possibilities to the limit. Developing their potential becomes a source of immense pleasure, and they feel no pain at all. Or if they do, that pain is also joy because, as Kenji taught us, for a poet who manifests his divine talents "even suffering is joy."

A Building for Kenji's School

The first Kenji's school to have its own building was established in September 1994. The building is located in Miasa-mura, a peaceful mountain village with a population of 1,300 in Kitaazumi-gun, Nagano Prefecture. Situated about 15 minutes' drive from Omachi Station on the JR Shinshu Line with a view of the Northern Japan Alps, it is a perfect location for communing with nature.

All of the students board at the school which has a limit of three semesters, each of which is six months in duration. At present there are eleven students. The building is an old school that for eighteen years housed an alternative school by the name of Yugakusha under the direction of Hitoshi Yoshida.

Although we only recently began operation, our students have already made surprising progress, maturing rapidly. The changes taking place have far exceeded our expectations.

At the Miasa School we include only those activities and subjects that are essential to our students' beings. If we attempt to impose non-essentials, the students will lose touch with their feelings, with what they want to do, becoming confused by inner conflict and anxiety. They will no longer be capable of directing their whole being toward nature and receiving its power. By offering instead only what they need, they are able to regain a rapport with their inner powers and heal themselves as all living creatures do.

About eleven o'clock one night a month or so after the school first opened, a thirteen-day-old moon, nearly full, rose in the sky. White frost descended on the grass that covers two-thirds of the schoolyard. We waded into the grass where the frost lay, and settled down for a lesson on watching the moon and the frost. Just one month before, we had sat in the same place and watched the dawn and the morning light on the dew, but moonlight on frost had its own special beauty. In the light of the moon, each tiny ice crystal shone with its own individual light, each had its own transparency, its own strength. As opposed to the red light of dawn, this was a field of blue lamplight cast by minute crystals of ice reflecting the indigo glow of the night. It was the light of the white clover in Kenji's work "*Polano no hiroba*" (Polano Square).

We were all deeply moved and as we sang Kenji's "*Hoshi meguri uta*" (The Star Tripping Song) our spirits rose and we could not stay still but simply had to dance. Our beings had gradually changed so that we now responded in this way.

About two and a half months after the school opened, a newspaper reporter came to interview me about the school. At noon it had been a clear sunny day but in the early evening the temperature suddenly dropped, and strong gusts of wind swept the red autumn leaves up into the sky in a boisterous revel. The trees on the mountainside began swaying none too gently, their leaves rustling, while the tall heads of the eulalia grasses sent up white flames and waves rolled across the surface of the meadow, transforming the entire scene into a single symphony. At that moment, the students with their burden of rice seedlings froze in their tracks, their attention riveted on the murmuring trees, their mouths hanging open in wonder.

"What results have you seen at your school in the last two and a half months?" the reporter asked. I simply pointed to the students standing in open-mouthed astonishment, completely absorbed in the movement of the trees and said, "That."

It was indeed a great result. Just as Kenji had seen nature as an expression of his own spirit, the same process was now beginning within these students.

When we begin to change in this way, we no longer need anything else. We can identify those things that are unnecessary, and begin to realize that a simpler lifestyle is better. If you go to a department store it may make you feel that the clothes you wear are shabby and cause you to crave for material things. But people who experience the beauty of light on the morning dew or of shining frost need nothing more. And they become capable of viewing themselves or the world from the perspective of what is truly essential. Once they reach this point, they will no longer be at the mercy of comparative evaluations or material desires, but will progress steadily forward.

In the end, refraining from the superfluous allows us to devote all our energy to the essential things in life. Accordingly, we no longer begrudge expending anything on what we need to manifest our talents, just as Kenji poured all his money into buying records. That is the type of person our students will become.

A School for Parents and Children

What concrete steps are we taking at Kenji's school to allow each person to learn what he or she needs?

First, we facilitate the kind of workshops mentioned previously to resolve the confusion within each person's being. When people are confused, they are incapable of judging what they really need to learn. Therefore, at Kenji's school, we encourage parents and children, married couples and siblings, to participate. If they approach Kenji's school with the intention of starting their lives over, they will come to clearly understand the problems that they need to resolve.

At present, we have one mother-son duo at our Miasa school. The son, who is completely blind, was prone to making such drastic pronouncements as, "Death to the Emperor!" when he first entered the school because of the influence of a religious cult. He was so sickly that he spent much of his time in the hospital and never felt truly well, and he even introduced himself by announcing that he was schizophrenic. He suffered from auditory hallucinations and his parents and other people around him were kept busy trying to suppress them with drugs, etc.

When I tried to explain to his mother that the anxiety within her child was actually an expression of the anxiety within her own self, she had trouble understanding. I therefore started working with her to identify the problem points in her own upbringing.

When her child was born blind, her parents condemned her, saying, "Such a child should not have been born to someone in our family," and she was pressured into leaving her home and the town she lived in. Although she herself was not conscious of it, she naturally harbored a great deal of anger against her parents.

She, too, however, blamed herself for her child's blindness, believing she had caused it by marrying against her parents' wishes and by overworking, and thought, "If only I hadn't married against their wishes. If only I hadn't worked so hard." And she believed that if only her child could see, everything would be resolved.

Her son felt that his mother had rejected him and his blindness while she, herself, remained oblivious of the enormous suffering she was causing him. Because he intuitively recognized that she could not accept him because he was blind, he was unable to accept himself, a condition that was extremely painful.

He wished that he could see because he believed that his mother would then accept him. But this was a wish that could never be fulfilled. He heard voices telling him, "Die, die. Hurry up and die! Die and then be reborn with healthy eyes." Those voices reflected his mother's subconscious thoughts.

I explained to her in the following manner.

You did not have a blind child because you married against your parents' wishes. Nor was he born that way because you overworked. There are many people who overwork. This child was born into the world through the will of the universe which has a power far exceeding your own will. And he chose you to be his mother.

All things in this world operate through this universal will. Sightless children, and children who can see, all are born as an expression of this will that transcends the power of man. People who can see lose something through the very capacity of sight, while those who are blind are capable of seeing what others cannot. Every single person exists in this world for a reason.

The fact that this child exists and that you are his mother is also the will of the universe. Certainly it may be difficult for you to relate to him. That is because you are blaming yourself and doing everything on your own. Moreover, because you are unable to accept the fact that you have borne a blind child, this child will never be able to accept his sightless self, has even rejected his own existence and fallen into confusion. That is why your life is so difficult. If you can understand the earnestness of this life force that chose you as the medium for his birth into this world, you will be filled with gratitude for the fact that he was born blind.

This in effect is what I said to her.

Subsequently, we worked together on expressing verbally the things she had wanted to say to her parents when she was a child. Her heart, which was deadened by pain and exhaustion, warmed to life through the expression of her true feelings and she stopped surrendering to apathy or blaming herself. At the same time, the voices that her child had been hearing completely ceased and he became bright and happy.

Recently this youth said to me, "The voices have changed. They just sound like happy music now. It's too bad because I was planning to do what you told me last time, that if I heard them again I should enjoy them and play with them, making them into a song."

"That is too bad," I said, very moved. This youth who had taken his mother's anxiety about his ability to live independently, her fears about what would happen to him if she died first, and made them his own, became completely transformed once his mother resolved her spiritual confusion. Mother and child were able to separate from each other and he returned to his classmates at the Miasa school. He developed relationships among the students and with nature and living things, and within these relationships his youthful heart began to grow. Not just his heart, but the hearts of all our students. This is what moved me. A further surprise was the fact that his mother began to manifest her own innate talents. She is now becoming involved in caring for emotionally damaged youths.

Having seen several cases of this type, I prefer whenever possible to have parents and children attend Kenji's school together. If they cannot attend the entire course, it is worthwhile to attend for even a week or a month and spend a block of time together. I believe that Kenji's school will be established as a place where people can reeducate and heal themselves to start life over.

Learning and Expressing with Your Being

At Kenji's school we place great importance on using one's entire being as part of the learning process.

Children who fail or fall behind in the regular school system are generally poor at abstract thinking but at the same time have an excellent grasp of things concrete. The lessons that I conducted in public school, whether the subject were language or mathematics, all consisted of translating abstract concepts into physical actions or visual objects that could be experienced and felt by the child, stimulating the cognitive process. When something is translated into concrete action, no matter what it is, the mechanism of the universe which is incorporated into the being of each child becomes manifest in mathematics or principles, in formulas, words, or diagrams.

A fifth grader in my homeroom class once asked me, "Teacher, what does 'plus' mean?" With the other children's assistance, I gave him various examples, using concrete actions to explain. "Ah," he said, "Now I understand. So then, what does 'minus' mean?" To be honest, I was astonished at first that a fifth grader would need to ask this question. But it was only in fifth grade that he had finally reached the point where he was capable of forming such a query.

Once, when I needed to use dice in class, he pointed to a picture of a die on the cover of his booklet of math problems and said, "Teacher, you can cut this out and use it."

"All right then. Cut it out and see," I said giving him my own copy. He began to cut but in the middle of the task it suddenly dawned on him that a two-dimensional picture of a die will not roll.

The joy this type of child experiences at such revelations is no trifling thing. The child's energy changes the atmosphere of the entire class and he begins to lead the other students. They are impressed by his discoveries and start to exclaim,

"Look what he can do now!" or "He thinks of things nobody else thought of." As they discover more, he will encourage them further with such declarations as, "We're all geniuses, aren't we?"

Some of the students at Kenji's school are either university graduates or currently enrolled in university. These students tend to rely on intellect alone, rarely having had an opportunity to experience or express things with their entire being. Through them we have been made painfully aware of the need for feeling and thinking through experience and for physical expression.

In order to express things physically, we must enrich and hone our senses. This requires physical training geared at recovering and sharpening the body's senses. For this reason, the Noguchi method, *eurythmy* (a compulsory subject in Steiner Schools in which music or words are expressed through movement), and *Ki* (an Oriental practice that uses breathing and posture to stimulate one's inner energy and maintain one's physical and mental balance) form an important part of our curriculum.

In the Noguchi method, for example, twelve body types are identified and we tailor our lessons to suit each different type. These types include people who experience fatigue because they always think and never act, those whose actions are dictated by their likes and dislikes, those who are motivated by the desire to win, those who act on intuition before they think, and vice versa. For each body type, we must consider what would best facilitate the manifestation of their God-given talents. The content of our lessons is never uniform, but rather is focused upon seeking the path that suits a particular individual.

Latent-consciousness education is another important component of the Noguchi method. Instead of working with a person on the conscious level, we approach the subconscious or latent consciousness. As Kenji says, "That which does not spring from the subconscious is impotent or a sham."

Human bodies come equipped with their own inherent healing power, and sickness is but a manifestation of this capacity. For example, catching a cold is simply the body's unconscious way of correcting some imbalance. A cold with a high fever causes the body to sweat and loosens any tightness, while at the same time killing unnecessary germs. Practicing the Noguchi method helps increase this natural healing power.

The Noguchi *yuki* method, in which the inner energy of a healthy person, or persons, is transmitted to a patient to cure an illness, has also been very effective in energy work. People long to have their existence recognized by others, and to this end, they transmit and receive a calming energy. The *yuki* method trains the body to tap this energy and because it helps us to know the condition of our own bodies and hearts, it is a key part of our curriculum.

We have neither a nurse's room nor a doctor at our school. Rather, each person works to develop the natural capacity to maintain his or her own health. If someone becomes ill and is unable to recover on his or her own, we transmit our collective energy to that person through the laying on of hands and by caring for the individual in various ways. So far, all instances of illness have been successfully cured in this way.

To do what you are capable of doing. This is an extremely important point. One of the greatest causes of the various ills in society today is our dependence on experts for things that we should be doing ourselves. We have relinquished our own responsibilities, relying instead on the school, the administration, the doctor. But by leaving everything in the hands of experts, the innate powers lying dormant within each of us remain untapped. Our hearts, too, remain dependent upon others. In this state, nothing can improve.

Recovering the Wild Side

Another major theme at Kenji's school is the recovery of our savage instincts. To do this, we must focus on the wildness that exists in nature.

A wasteland, for example, is only a wasteland from the perspective of one who cultivates rice. Looked at from nature's point of view, "wasteland" is land to which health has been restored by the return of nature's fierce vitality, its life force.

It is a mistake to assume that nature is kind to humans. Nature controlled by humans is kind to humans, and if you think about it, this is an emasculated form in which the natural power of life has been modified for the convenience of humankind. There may be some aspects of nature that appear kind to us, but they always conceal the risk of mortal danger.

At Kenji's school, we believe that it is necessary to experience risk, by spending, for example, a few days alone in the mountains. This allows us to see ourselves as a part of nature. It also enables us to recover our savage instincts which demand that we protect our own lives.

Several times we have used the gymnasium or other venue for one or two days to conduct an entertaining course called "living in the hunting and gathering age." The class is separated into hunters and hunted, and without exception, each person makes a variety of energizing and invigorating discoveries. Many, for example, expect that captured prey will experience death and consumption as painful. To their surprise, they discover it to be pleasant. Similarly, others find themselves reevaluating the meaning of killing. The experience thus forces participants to reconsider everything that they perceive to be common sense. More importantly, they begin to recall memories of the hunting and gathering age which are imprinted in their being. They recover the physical senses from that period when man ran barefoot between thorny thickets through field and mountain, knowing that he might, at any moment, encounter and fall prey to another beast, or from the time when he conversed with various creatures, with the plants and the stars.

I have been in many life-threatening situations since my childhood, have placed myself in circumstances where death would be a natural outcome, so I know the importance of such lessons. But the response to this course far exceeded my expectations.

When I implemented similar lessons during my career as a schoolteacher, the response was so enthusiastic that I decided to try it with parents and children who similarly became totally absorbed. They built barricades to protect themselves, hunted and were hunted, until at last the creatures were caught. Prayer rituals were performed and the captured prey experienced the ecstasy of being eaten. This extraordinary experience which upsets commonly accepted ethical values frees the participants from the bonds of common sense, thereby activating their savage nature. During this short period of time, it is possible to experience one's own wildness.

One essential element that we have incorporated into this particular course is confronting one's own death. It is the undefined fear of death that causes people to cling to various religions. This fear drives some people to amass spiritual "property" through, for example, membership in a sect that promises salvation, as a safety blanket in case of emergencies. If we confront death, however, we become aware of the preciousness of living and are awakened to the essential meaning of life.

Another aspect of death that we have been working on at Kenji's school is creating bonds with the dead. We do not sever ourselves from those who have died. We also establish connections with animals and plants that have died to support human life, and with water and air that have been defiled purely for the sake of human convenience. By making connections, we create a continuum from the past to the future, and it becomes possible to view the world and our own existence within that context. We understand more broadly and deeply what Kenji means by "the world" in his exhortation for us to realize "the happiness of the world."

Absorbing the Power of Nature and the Universe

A leaflet advertising *The Restaurant of Many Orders*, a collection of his stories, includes a quote from Kenji's writings that particularly captures the significance of his works.

Iiwatov is the name of a place. Should you seek that place, consider it to be the same world as the field tilled by Big and Little Klaus, or the land through the looking glass visited by the little girl, Alice, far east of the Even Kingdom, and northeast of the Tepantal Desert. This is the dreamland of Iwate, Japan, scenes which actually exist like this in my heart. There anything is possible. A person can fly in an instant across the icy snow and follow the circulating wind on a northward journey, or speak with an ant crawling beneath a red flower cup. There even sin and sorrow shine with pure beauty. Deep forest groves, wind and shadow, the evening primrose, or a strange metropolis and rows of telegraph poles that stretch as far as Bering City; it is indeed a mysterious and wonderful land. This collection of tales is but a sampling of some of my mental sketches which are presented in the form of literature for adolescents nearing the end of their childhood years.

If I were to describe the features of this collection from this perspective, they could be set down in the following points:

1. These tales have taken the seeds of truth and await the beauty of their germination. They are not, by any means, the dregs of worn-out existing religions or morals that have been disguised to deceive the pure of heart.

2. Their purpose is to offer the materials to make a new, a better world; but one which is a development of our own world, concerning the progress of which the author himself is ignorant and at which he constantly marvels. It is certainly not some trumped-up, twisted, soot-colored utopia.

3. These tales are neither counterfeit nor fiction. Nor are they stolen. Although there may have been some reflection or analysis, this is truly how they appeared within my heart at the time. Therefore, no matter how ridiculous or how unintelligible they may be, they will strike a common chord within the hearts of all people. They will be virtually incomprehensible to dishonest adults.

4. They are produce fresh from country fields and gardens. We offer you these mental sketches along with the green vegetables and glossy fruit born of wind and light in the countryside.

This description is not restricted only to the works contained in *The Restaurant of Many Orders*. I think that by reading this, anyone can understand what moved Kenji to write, and how his works are indeed an expression of his divine talents. The preface to *The Restaurant of Many Orders* introduced previously is a simpler, easy-to-understand explanation of the same.

When he states that "This collection of tales is but a sampling of some of my mental sketches," he is referring not to superficial consciousness but rather to his subconscious mind, and from this one can glean that the will of the universe and the laws of the galaxy were revealed within his heart.

His spirit, his imagination could travel anywhere and become anything. What a free, a phantasmagoric existence.

Imaging is also given special importance at Kenji's school. Students transpose images that embody meaning for them personally, those inspired by words or music, or those expressed in actions, pictures, or words, into literature or pictures, dance or music, stories or poetry.

Kenji believed that the power to create a new age exists within the universe, within nature. He felt it with his being and then expressed it. As he states in his own words,

My attention is drawn to the clouds,
  to the wind,
Not simply as a concept
But because they are an inexhaustible source of power,
Power for a new people.

"A new people" refers to those who will establish a new world, one that differs from that of the present materialistic age. The clouds and the wind will provide the source of power, as of course they empowered Kenji himself. Verses such as "Translucent power, Of cloud and wind, Infuse this youth" from the poem "That Field Over There, You See" or

"With all your might, Play the pipe organ of light, That fills the sky" from "Valediction" aptly express this man who received the power to live, the power to find his direction in life from nature.

Light and Darkness and a Healthy Being

Kenji directed his attention not only to the light but to the darkness as well. At Kenji's school, likewise, we examine those things that are generally considered "don'ts" and include them in our lessons. We free ourselves from incantations of the various rules and values that maintain society, such as do not kill, do not steal, do not break, do not lie, do not bully.

By incorporating them into our lessons, I do not mean that we actually commit such acts. Rather, we use Kenji's literature.

There are many examples of bullying in his works. He exposes the numerous evils we hide in our hearts, depicting people enraged by jealousy, or boasting, or acting proud and haughty, scenes of suicide or violent murder or someone convincing a victim, while killing him, that it is for his own good. Enacting such episodes can effectively release the forbidden, the ugly, the unfashionable, and the vulgar that we have locked away. Through repeated group dramatizations of Kenji's works, by reading them with our entire being, we are able to accept the dark side of ourselves which we had previously suppressed. And in so doing, the darkness is no longer darkness alone. That part of ourselves which was confined within as darkness and denied life is revived and freed, fusing with light. Within this struggle between light and darkness, our beings become oriented toward self-development.

This deeply buried part of the self that is exposed by confronting the inner Ashura or darkness is directly related to our will to live. Through that confrontation, a dynamic sense of life is born, one in which the self exists and interconnects with others. When implementing actual workshops, it becomes clear that health cannot be restored by concentrating only on one side to the exclusion of the other. When light is connected to darkness and vice versa, our beings are filled with energy and, like a wilted plant revived by water, our vitality is magically restored.

One of the defects in the education system today is that it categorizes things as right or wrong, suppressing the latter. What is the standard for distinguishing right from wrong, good from bad, beautiful from ugly, superior from inferior? One of our tasks at Kenji's school is to reevaluate those things that have been determined simply to suit the convenience of society, by sifting them through our beings.

The fact that Kenji himself did not judge people and society by existing standards has already been touched upon in previous comments concerning "Kenju's Wood" and "Wildcat and the Acorns."

There is a story in Hanamaki about two men named Ben and Toku who were considered fools. No one in the town ever greeted them except Kenji, who bowed to them. Whenever he did, they would happily report, "Today we worshiped Kenji." These two, who lived in tune with the rhythm of heaven and never concerned themselves with distinguishing who was superior and who was not, felt respect for and fellowship with Kenji precisely because he operated on the same wavelength as they.

Focusing on Both the Light and the Darkness

I believe that the reason Kenji felt the darkness within himself much more strongly than others was because of the training he received from his parents and the influence of Buddhist scriptures.

Once his mother complained to his siblings, saying, "Why does Kenji never think about himself? He's always doing things for others."

"But Mother," they exclaimed, "he's only doing what you have always told us to."

"Oh. I see."

This anecdote indicates that these principles were an integral part of daily life in the Miyazawa family. Both his parents were devout Buddhists, although his father was strict while his mother was extremely gentle and kind. When he was teaching, Kenji staged a dramatic performance at the school and invited the students who had performed to his home afterwards. His mother was also there and she served each one of them assiduously. "She was just like a living Buddha," Toshio Nagasaka recollected.

His mother's gentleness intermingled with the teachings of Buddha nurturing the roots of Kenji's heart. It followed naturally that he was severe with regard to his own Ashura. The more his concern for others deepened, the more his severity toward himself increased.

From his childhood, Kenji's kindness was legendary. One famous anecdote relates that when a friend was made to stand in the corridor holding a bucket of water as a form of punishment, Kenji felt such sympathy for him that he drank all the water in the bucket. At the same time, he never fled from facing the Ashura within himself. Like the law of action and reaction, his longing for purity was born precisely because he confronted them.

In his poem "*Seishinka*" (Song of the Spirit), Kenji proclaims:

> The sun reigns and the dazzling light of
>   the solar system is at mid-day.
> In the midst of an arduous journey
> We tread the path of light.

Because the existence of the Ashura weighs heavily within him, he treads the path of light and journeys in search of the sacred, of true nobility. Of all his desires, this one was especially strong.

In the same way, to fix one's gaze on both the light and the darkness, rather than on one or the other, is to acknowledge one's very existence and is prerequisite for manifesting one's true powers. One of the central themes we must tackle at Kenji's school is the incorporation of this element into our studies.

As Numerous as the Stars

We also place great importance on the study of molecular, atomic, elementary particles and electromagnetic physics as fields that explain at the micro level all existing things on this planet and in the universe. Likewise, we need to study cytology and microbiology. All are important tools for understanding the composition of our bodies as well as for understanding the connections between different phenomena and elucidating the process of recycling matter into earth, air, or water.

An understanding of cosmic and planetary physics is essential if we are to comprehend the origin of the universe, as are geology and soil science. And in order to glimpse the mysteries of the universe and the four-dimensional world in which time and space are united, we will need to study, among other things, the theory of relativity.

Of course, we must also acquire a basic knowledge of such familiar things as clothing, food, and shelter, part of which will entail studying the recycling of discarded items. And needless to say we must include the study of the arts and human history in various fields. Every subject is in the end related to developing our hearts and beings.

When he took his students to Iwate Mountain, Kenji suddenly leapt into the air, shouting "Hoho!", grabbed the mechanical pencil that hung from a string around his neck and scribbled something on a piece of paper, tossed the paper aside, picked it up to write again, then threw it down, and leapt from rock to rock shouting "Hoho!" as if he were not quite human. One student, Kudo, was frightened, believing that his teacher had gone mad. Toshio Nagasaka explains that this was how he behaved whenever he had a flash of inspiration, and it is certain that his being had a capacity for sensitive rapport with nature, leaping from the mundane world into another space entirely when enlightened. As has been repeatedly stated, the development of such sensitivity and the nurturing of our capacity for honest rapport with nature is considered vital at Kenji's school. Kenji's written works are important textbooks for our students. Monkey, deer, and a variety of other animals inhabit the area around Miasa-mura. You can imagine how moving it was to encounter a deer in the mountains after reading Kenji's "*Shishiodori no hajimari*" (The First Deer Dance). Likewise, reading "*Saru no koshikake*" (The Monkey Seat) after seeing a group of monkeys makes for a completely different type of appreciation.

In addition, Kenji's works are a treasure trove of words, from the names of animals to scientific terms from all different fields. It is fascinating to use the opportunities his writings provide to study the original meaning of words.

Let me take this opportunity to introduce the *jugend* seminar that we conduct at the school. This seminar is designed for those who cannot develop their innate talents and who are unable to find satisfaction in life. Many of us have so lost touch with our beings that we remain oblivious of that loss, unable to be our true selves, trying instead to live up to the evaluations or expectations of others.

People such as this must first be placed in a slow-moving time frame. For most of those who come to the school, having time for themselves is a new experience. They turn their eyes inward, focusing steadily on their self, identifying the problems that exist within their heart or body and what it is that they really seek, listening to this voice with their whole being. They search earnestly until their being is satisfied that it knows what it wants to do, what it is best suited to do.

The *jugend* seminar is not only for *jugend* ("youth") but for all who wish to quietly and deeply contemplate their selves, regardless of age, for all who want to manifest their potential to the fullest. In Japan, where making a living is considered the first condition of maturity while self-determination and human development are ignored, most people are enslaved by money-making jobs, neglecting their spiritual growth and consequently the emptiness within their hearts has become a yawning chasm. Our school, however, welcomes all who have refused to give up hope completely and who long to change this pattern.

Through such activities as the *jugend* seminar, they can absorb the spirit of Kenji and seek a way to utilize that spirit in the present. We aim to create as many such schools in the world as there are stars in the sky, schools that provide a space to realize the goals Kenji describes in *An Introduction to Peasant Art*, seeking happiness for the whole world and transforming our daily lives into the realm of fourth-dimensional art.

We are all peasants; industrious, our work gruelling.

We seek a path to a brighter, fresher life.

There were a few such as this among the masters of old.

I wish to consider this in the context of the union of modern scientific proofs, the experience of the truthseekers, and our intuition.

The happiness of the individual cannot be attained without first realizing the happiness of the whole world.

The concept of self will gradually evolve from the individual to include the group, society, and finally the universe.

Is this not the same path as that followed and taught by the saints of old?

The new age will be found where the world becomes one consciousness and a single, living entity.

To live strongly and truly is to live in awareness of the galaxy within you and to respond to it.

Let us seek true happiness for the whole world; the search itself is the path.

At Kenji's school we use our hands, our feet, our head, our entire body to relearn and accumulate the wisdom necessary for building the coming era.

We aim for self-sufficiency, raising our own crops and livestock, receiving the bounty of the sky, the mountains, and the rivers, and emphasizing the importance of making things with our own hands such as pottery, charcoal, houses, and furniture. In addition, we express our beings through music, art, recitation, and drama, to develop an awareness of the unconscious pressures that dominate us, and work to establish our own selves.

The objectives of the *jugend* seminar can be summarized in the following four points.

1. The acquisition of a variety of manual skills and the

ability to live self-sufficiently anywhere in the world and to enjoy life without being controlled by money.

2. The development of the ability to create relationships in which one can be one's self and foster mutual development within a communal environment, the ability to create relationships that nurture mutual growth.

3. The training of one's being to relate to nature, learn from it, and receive its power, thereby learning about the world.

4. The development of the ability to care for one's own spirit and body, and to become independent of doctors, medicine, etc.

Our earnest desire is that all individuals will learn to live without comparing themselves to others, will manifest the talents and capacities entrusted to them from heaven, will learn together how to attain the happiness of the whole world, how to make possible the realization of a society that lives in connection with all living creatures on this planet. We want to acquire the power for ceaseless effort so that, over successive generations, we may create a society such as mankind has never before created.

The spirit of our school is perfectly expressed in Kenji's *An Introduction to Peasant Art*:

...Friends! Let us join our righteous power, and combine all our lands, our lives, to create a single magnificent fourth-dimensional art...

The vast stage of human life revolves about the axis of time to create an imperishable fourth-dimensional art.

Friends! You must go. Soon all will follow...

...What is required of us is a crystalline will encompassing the galaxy, enormous power and fervor...

For a poet, even suffering is joy.

The eternally incomplete is in itself complete.

When schools based on the spirit of Kenji's words become as numerous as the stars, human society will undoubtedly give birth to a productive, spiritual society that is far removed from the materialistic society of today. The future will surely unfold as Kenji foretold. And when it does, Kenji will beam down upon us from the far end of the universe.

Afterword—About Kenji's School

Kenji Miyazawa is the number one seller in modern Japanese literature. He is so well known that to use a common Japanese expression, he is considered a "national author." But there is no one to whom such an expression is less suited than Kenji. During his lifetime, he rarely received any royalties or recognition as a writer or a poet, and moreover, he was completely indifferent to any "nation"-like grouping. For Kenji, who, if it were possible, would have published poetry collections in the languages of frogs, birch trees, or the wind, nothing could have seemed more ridiculous than conforming to human frameworks, let alone those of the Japanese nation.

A large portion of his works were written to be read to his students or for them to perform. Despite the number of his books being sold, I wonder whether people are actually reading them as they were intended to be read. I myself know very well how long I spent reading his works superficially, sitting at my desk, at a loss to understand his appeal.

In my case, enlightenment occurred when I read a short poem entitled "Regardless of What Others May Say." As this poem has already been introduced in the main text, I will not repeat it here. It is a simple poem insisting that the author is, regardless of what others may say, a young elaeagnus. When I read this poem out loud, the power of those words transformed me into an elaeagnus tree. I could see the clouds, the ridgeline from the tree's perspective; I could feel the freshness of the dew, the wind passing between my branches, the warmth of the earth at my feet. It seemed that Kenji was staring at me absently, but that figure became myself. I was the elaeagnus; I was Kenji watching the elaeagnus; I was Kenji becoming the elaeagnus; I was myself looking at myself as the elaeagnus. And this seemed perfectly natural.

Since then, his poems, which I had previously thought to be incomprehensible, have never failed to make me feel the breeze caressing my skin. His words are a guidebook to the planet, and I realized that if I but followed them I could go anywhere and be anything. Although a pale comparison to the forests of Kenji's Iwate, in the woods remaining on Mount Rokko near Kobe I discovered that I could become an oak, a granite stone, a clod of earth beneath a pile of fallen leaves, or succulent moss. I had already been practicing *Ki* for many years and Kenji's poetry seemed to increase the receptivity of my being. Kenji seems to have been a natural master of *Ki* who could hear the spirit of wind and cloud, of frogs and pebbles, and translate these into the poetry of men.

Toshiko Toriyama's being is highly attuned to this facet of Kenji. Where scholars read his works with their minds, she reads them with her being, a being born and bred in the bountiful nature of Shikoku where she spent her childhood; a being with thirty years' experience struggling to help children retain their receptivity; a being the sensitivity of which has been polished through methods employed by the Takauchi Drama Research Center and Noguchi *seitai*. In her, one can clearly glimpse the being of Kenji which fuses with nature and is compelled to take on the great work of heaven which far exceeds the limitations of the times and the common sense of society. When approached in this way, Kenji's works begin to shine and we catch a glimpse of what he longed to do as an educator.

I am very glad that this book is being published in commemoration of the hundredth anniversary of Kenji's birth which is attracting widespread attention. Without this book I feel that Kenji will be commercialized as an author, reduced to a mere commodity. Instead, through the medium of Toshiko Toriyama's being, we have access to Kenji as an irreplaceable elder brother for those men who suffer because they are on a different wavelength from that of their workplace, for those women who are exhausted from the struggle against the tangible and intangible violence directed at them by their husbands, and for children floundering in the mire of competition and bullying at this, the end of the twentieth century marked by the Hanshin earthquake, Aum Supreme Truth's sarin gas attacks, and the Monju nuclear accident. I am not trying to evaluate or criticize Kenji, nor do I want to deify him. His literature simply helps me, personally, to release my frigid, restricted being, allowing it to grow freely until its receptivity reaches the clouds. It has nothing to do with being superior or inferior. Kenji's school has come into being precisely because this is such a crucial issue at this time. The name, like Steiner or Neils, is incidental. It could just as easily be called the school for humankind, the school of creation, or the people's school.

Our goal of establishing as many Kenji's schools as there are stars in the sky may sound like a dream. But this is no ideological movement seeking to expand the number of its adherents. Nor is it a profit-oriented chain-store type development. Rather, it is a call to create and mutually support a place that nurtures life for parents, children, and teachers who have become aware of the Kenji-like receptivity their beings possess and who want to pool their learning. Therefore it is only natural to begin with a number equivalent to the number of people who have come into contact with, and whose beings have been moved by, Kenji's literature. This is not that difficult for anybody. Simply reading his works aloud, using gestures to express them with your being can spark myriad inspirations; as Toshiko Toriyama says, "like children, like primitive people." This cannot be learned from the external but rather must be recollected from within. I hope that this book will spark many things within you as you read it.

Takashi Tsumura

The Author:Toshiko Toriyama

Born in Hiroshima prefecture, Japan in 1941, Toshiko Toriyama discovered her attitude toward life in the poem "*Ame Nimo Makezu*" (Never stopped by rain) written by Kenji Miyazawa. In 1964, she began working as a public school teacher and strove throughout her career to develop a more human approach to education. She resigned in 1994 and since then has devoted her energies to establishing Kenji's school, traveling throughout Japan.

The Translator:Cathy Hirano

Cathy Hirano was born in Canada and has lived in Japan since 1978. She has translated several books, including *The Friends* by Kazumi Yumoto, which was awarded the Mildred Bachelder Award in 1997 as one of the most outstanding books translated into English for publication in the United States.

International Foundation for the Promotion of Languages and Culture (IFLC)

Purpose and Background

The International Foundation for the Promotion of Languages and Culture (IFLC) —a non-profit corporation approved by the Ministry of Education, Culture, and Science of Japan on June 20, 1995— was founded in order to promote linguistic and cultural exchange all over the world through a donation from Sunmark Inc.

With the 21st century close at hand, Japan's role in the world is becoming more and more important. In these circumstances, cultural and linguistic exchange in particular is going to be focused on more, and it is very urgent to nurture people who can handle several languages including English and to promote cultural exchange widely all over the world. On the other hand, many nations, including developing countries, expect an interchange of personnel with Japan, and we need to take a positive initiative to aid and promote mutual understanding.

Our work is to translate and introduce Japanese literature all over the world, translate and introduce excellent literature of other countries to Japan, aid or nurture highly trained translators in various languages, offer scholarships for students all over the world, sponsor seminars for language learning, and hold translation proficiency examinations. Through this constant public work, our aim is to contribute to the promotion of linguistic and cultural exchange and mutual understanding all over the world. And we believe that publication of works such as this is our role to promote cultural exchange and mutual understanding all over the world.

Keiichi Kajikawa, Chairman,IFLC

Kenji's School
—Ideal Education for All
（英語版　賢治の学校）

1997年5月30日　初版印刷
1997年6月15日　初版発行

著者　鳥山敏子
訳者　平野キャシー

発行人　椛川恵一
発行所　財団法人　国際言語文化振興財団
〒169　東京都新宿区高田馬場1-32-13
サンマークビル

発売元　株式会社　サンマーク
〒169　東京都新宿区高田馬場1-32-13
サンマークビル
TEL:03-5272-3166　FAX:03-5272-3167

印刷　（株）共同印刷
製本　村上製本所

ISBN4-7631-9187 C0030